ORIGINAL TRAUMA

ORIGINAL TRAUMA

The Story of Inherited Generational Trauma in the Bible

by
Ramon K. Jusino

Ramon K. Jusino Services, LLC
Publishing Division
Staten Island, New York

Cover Art:
The Sacrifice of Isaac
Orazio Riminaldi (1593-1630)

The author is not responsible for websites cited herein (or their content) that are not owned by the author.

The author is not a mental healthcare professional. This book is not a substitute for professional therapy or counseling.

All biblical quotations taken from
The King James Version of the Bible.

Published in the United States of America

ISBN 979-8-9882395-1-2

Library of Congress Control Number: 2023907609

Ramon K. Jusino Services, LLC
Publishing Division
P.O. Box 100073
Staten Island, NY 10310

First Edition

To my lovely wife, Ann, who is the inspiration for much of the good that I try to do—and to our two wonderful children, William and Hannah, whom I hope I have not wounded too much with of any of the generational trauma I've inherited and passed on to them.

And in memory of Ramon and Mariana, who were loving parents to my sisters and myself under some very difficult circumstances. They were the pastors of our domestic church. They were our first teachers. They were the first to teach us about Jesus. May their souls, through the mercy of God, rest in peace.

CONTENTS

"I form the light, and create darkness: I make peace, and create evil: I the LORD do all these things."
                                        -- Isaiah 45:7

PREFACE

———

WHETHER YOU BELIEVE in God or not, whether you believe in the Bible or not, the matters I discuss in this book concern *you*. Today, there is much discussion about inherited generational trauma, also known as inherited family trauma, intergenerational trauma, and transgenerational trauma.[1] Research shows that trauma experienced by our parents, grandparents, great-grandparents...etc., can be passed down so that it affects us today. Generational trauma is among the root causes of most of this world's ills.

Generational trauma can be passed down in two ways: (1) By parents through the modeling of their own behavior at home for their children to see, and/or (2) a genetic marking phenomenon known as epigenetics,[2] which is a process by which trauma can leave a chemical mark on a person's genes, which is then passed along to their children, grandchildren, and subsequent generations biologically.

Generational trauma involves all of us, to one extent or another, without exception. We were all brought up by imperfect parents or other caretakers. Even those of us who were fortunate enough to have been brought up by parents who loved us and meant well have—without doubt—been traumatized as children because we were raised by parents who suffered their own traumatic experiences as children, and then passed their trauma down to us.

Sigmund Freud (1856-1939),[3] the father of psychology and psychoanalysis, pioneered the idea that events in our childhood greatly influence our lives and shape who we become as adults.[4] Psychoanalysis, even today, is largely based on exploring one's childhood and

1

one's relationship with one's parents. So, the idea that our upbringing can subconsciously affect our mental health as adults is not new. Freud was saying this over one hundred years ago. But, as we shall see, the authors of the Bible, in their own way, made this same observation thousands of years before Freud.

***

There's an inspiring and compelling epic saga within the pages of the Holy Bible about how people from the earliest days of recorded human civilization began to wonder about the lives which they had found themselves living. As a people, they looked around at their world to find both a paradisical Eden, and a frightful place filled with all kinds of ominous occurrences of both natural and human-made origin. They began to ask what this world was all about. Why were they here? Where did they come from? What was the meaning of their lives? The people I speak of lived during, what historians would later call, the Bronze Age. While most people were concerned only with their day-to-day troubles and concerns, there emerged a class within their societies who were thinkers, i.e., people who concerned themselves with thoughts that were deeper and more profound than those of most. This was not a situation that is different from what we have today. These ancient thinkers had questions—many, many questions. Collectively, those deeper thinkers looked towards the heavens above with wonder. They felt alone in a world they did not understand. Receiving no answers to their questions at first, they experienced a collective existential crisis thousands of years before that term would be coined.

Their search for meaning in life began.

For a time, their search for meaning led them to believe that their world was created and run by a multitude of supernatural beings which eventually became known as gods. These gods were the creation of human imagination. These gods resembled human beings, and often displayed base human qualities and traits. These gods were credited with controlling natural phenomena such as storms, earthquakes, famines, and plagues. These gods needed to be placated and humored.

These gods dispensed rewards and punishments in ways that seemed arbitrary and capricious.

These ancient people felt the need to try to figure out how to please these gods so that the gods would be contented and, therefore, provide a better life experience for them. They developed systems of offerings and sacrifices and such for the gods. Leaders among them emerged who seemed to have special knowledge about how to please these gods. These leaders quickly became the only conduits between a fearful people and their gods. This gave rise to a then nascent concept—organized religion. Leaders of the first organized religions began to exploit the fears of believers. They told people that the gods demanded tribute in exchange for their kindness and benevolence. This worked like a cosmic protection racket.

Within this group of ancient peoples, with their burgeoning religious beliefs, emerged an even deeper thinking group that would eventually cause the polytheism in which they believed to become a henotheism, then eventually a monotheism. Belief in one God emerged. Specifically, this one God became identified as the God initially revealed to one man. This man lived in the ancient near east some 4,000 years ago. This man became known as the patriarch, Abraham. This group of which I speak is, of course, the people first known as the Israelites (the sons of Jacob, a.k.a. Israel), and later known as the Jews (the sons of Judah).

To this day, believers and followers of Judaism, Christianity, and Islam—that's some 55% of the world's population—all point to this one man, Abraham, as their spiritual father. In fact, the name Abraham means "father of many." Abraham became the father of many indeed.

***

As keen observers of the world around them, the authors of the Bible noticed many things. One of the things they observed is that, while they all aspired to live carefree and happy lives, their lives were instead filled abidingly with fear and trauma. They also observed that they often passed down the trauma and fear they experienced to their children and their grandchildren. They could see the pattern. Without the benefit of the knowledge of DNA or modern psychology, they observed that certain negative traits seemed to pass down from parent to child.

Like father like son. The sins of the fathers to the third and fourth generation. Their childhood relationships with their parents affected their adult lives.

While my focus in this book is on family inherited trauma, the fact is that childhood trauma can come from many sources. Children deal not only with their parents, they have siblings to deal with in most cases, extended family, family friends, neighbors, teachers, clergy, classmates, all of whom can be sources of trauma which can be passed on through the generations. Children also go through traumatic experiences that can scar them for life, which are not anybody's fault at all, such as the deaths of loved ones.

***

Our childhood homes are where we first learn certain basics about life. Many of the things we conclude about life as children can be damaging to our mental health, and affect us negatively into adulthood. This is known fact. Our first relationships are with our parents/caretakers and our siblings. These relationships go on to define, in our minds, all of our relationships with others as adults. We can develop skewed and harmful ideas about people and relationships which can reach into our adult lives and cause us all kinds of problems.

Our childhood homes are where most people get their first impressions of God. The childhood home can be said to be our first church. Because of this, if we grow up in a home with any degree of dysfunctionality—and who doesn't?—we can develop skewed and harmful ideas about God, which can also cause us all kinds of problems as adults.

After growing up in homes where we learned skewed and harmful ideas about people, relationships, and God—we grow up and want to have children of our own, so we can pass along everything *we* learned as children, to them. It takes a great deal of self-awareness to realize that we have been traumatized, and to not pass on the trauma we've inherited to our children.

Most of us cannot expect to rise above our own inherited trauma without help. In addition to identifying inherited generational trauma, the Bible also explicitly provides a roadmap for overcoming it. I'm not saying that Scripture should be a replacement for any professional help that people who experienced childhood trauma may need in order to deal with the fallout from trauma—such as depression, anxiety and such. But the roadmap in the Bible may be helpful in conjunction with therapy, in the same way that the reliance on a Higher Power is used in most twelve step programs.

***

When I refer to the Bible or the Scriptures, I mean the Judeo-Christian Scriptures known to many Christians as the Old and the New Testaments. Unless otherwise specified, when I refer to the Church, I refer to the Roman Catholic Church, of which I am a member.

What I hope to convey, especially to those who may not value the Bible at all, is respect for the people who wrote, compiled, and preserved the Bible. It contains humanity's earliest attempts to find meaning and purpose in life. I think we can all respect that, regardless of what our own religious viewpoints may be. Their efforts were commendable. The fact that the Bible is still the most widely sold and distributed book in the world speaks for itself. We don't have to accept everything the Bible says. But there is much wisdom in there which can be helpful for everybody, regardless of religious persuasion.

What I tell here—or rather merely point out—is an epic story that unfolds within the pages of Scripture about inherited generational trauma. You'll see it for yourself. In the story, generations of people went through life traumatized as children by their parents, and by what their parents taught them to believe about God. The people of the Bible believed in a God who explicitly said he wanted to be feared. He instilled such fear through actions such as a worldwide flood, killing firstborn sons, actually giving people diseases such as leprosy, killing entire towns, committing what we would refer to today as genocide, encouraging war after war…etc. All of this is found in Scripture. People went on to be, in effect, traumatized by God. But, as we shall see, they weren't actually traumatized by God. They were traumatized by their own *impressions* of God.

***

This book is a journey and a fresh look at this largely untold story of inherited generational trauma in the Bible. Each of us has our own impressions of God. Many don't believe that God even exists. But even atheists have their impressions of God.

The truths contained in this book are *my* truths, i.e., my opinions. I invite you to consider my truths and accept or reject them as you will. Some of my truths might challenge how you currently see God and the Bible. This might challenge or affect your current understanding of God. That's OK. One of the purposes of this book is to encourage you to think. Think for yourself. Fair warning though. Once certain things are pointed out to you, there's no unseeing them. There may be no turning back. If you're OK with that, read on.

I could do something corny at this point like show you a red pill and a blue pill and tell you that if you don't want to go any further then just take the blue pill and forget all about this. …But, nah, just read the book.

***

Our story begins with the collective existential crisis which inspired the world's first authors to write.

CHAPTER ONE

THE EXISTENTIAL CRISIS THAT STARTED IT ALL

"For in much wisdom is much grief:
and he that increaseth knowledge increaseth sorrow."
-- Ecclesiastes 1:18

————

WHAT IS THE meaning of life? This is perhaps the most basic of the existential questions. What's this life all about? And by "all" I mean the whole thing, the big picture, the grand scheme, the whole kit and caboodle.

The earliest known work of literature in the world is an epic poem from ancient Sumer—modern day Iraq—known as *The Epic of Gilgamesh*.[1] The best and most complete version of this work is the Standard Babylonian version discovered in 1853. This is considered to be the definitive version of *Gilgamesh*. It is said to date back to as early as 1300 B.C. *The Epic of Gilgamesh* is the world's first known piece of meaningful literature. It deals with gods, and the mystery of human mortality. After learning how to write things down, what inspired the first authors of creative literature were the mysteries of the meaning of life. As soon as they were able to write words on clay tablets, they went right to work. Their thoughts and ideas couldn't wait for paper and pen, typewriters, the printing press, and computer word processing. They had meaningful things to express and they needed to do it in writing. I think many writers can relate to this.

It is clear that *The Epic of Gilgamesh* was known to the authors of the Bible.[2] In *Gilgamesh*, a man is created from the soil by a god, lives naked among the animals, is tempted by a woman whom a god created for him, the man accepts food from the woman, and has to leave his original setting, unable to return. There is a snake who steals a plant of immortality from Gilgamesh. In *Gilgamesh*, the gods flood the earth and help one chosen individual and his family to survive it. A big link between the ancient Sumerians and the people of the Bible is the biblical patriarch—Abraham. Scripture tells us that Abraham originally came from Ur, a major Sumerian city-state. *Genesis 11:31*.[3] Given the fact that Abraham is acknowledged as the primary patriarch of all of the people of the Bible, it should come as no surprise that the Bible is so influenced by ancient Sumerian thought.

Some 3,000 years before Kierkegaard, Nietzsche, Sartre and others tackled existential questions,[4] early thinkers in the ancient Near East began pondering, contemplating, meditating, and praying about life in new ways. Many of their thoughts are still relevant and meaningful even by today's standards. These ancients first handed down their most sacredly held beliefs, values, and familial tribal folklore through oral tradition from generation to generation. The stories, teachings, laws, advice, wisdom, prayers, and impressions of God that they handed down were first put in writing by ancient Sumerians in *The Epic of Gilgamesh*, and then eventually collected, written, updated, and compiled by ancient Israelites into what would become known to billions as The Holy Bible. The Bible is their legacy. The Bible is the inheritance they passed down to us. It is an impressive legacy, to say the least.

At some point, very early on in history, these human beings from among the earliest civilizations felt compelled to move beyond the Darwinian mandate to simply survive and reproduce. They began to ask the larger questions. They began to ponder the meaning of life on levels beyond that of their ancestors. They wondered what it was all about.

If the Bible seems confusing, contradictory, or even offensive at times, that's because it contains the impressions about God and life from people who were just beginning to try to figure it all out. The Bible contains accounts about, and from, the earliest prophets, i.e., people who claimed to speak for God. These prophets intended to impart truth. But did, say, the prophet Moses have *all* the answers? Absolutely not. If so, there would have been no need for any subsequent prophets after him. But many subsequent prophets would come. Each of them modified, expanded, and sometimes gently corrected the teachings of Moses. The image of God presented throughout the Bible was a work in progress. That's the best way to look at it. Each prophet and each Bible writer sought, in their own way—under what they believed to be the inspiration of God—to deepen the understanding of God among their people. It was a noble cause. It was a noble effort.

We, and our impressions of God today, are *still* a work in progress.

***

The existential questions I referred to are actually posed throughout the Bible in one way or another. Most people still don't have satisfying answers to these questions even today. I wonder how many of us walk around with an underlying and unacknowledged angst about the mysteries and uncertainties of our lives as we understand them. This world can be a confusing place. There are no easy answers to its complexities.

When people have questions about the meaning of life, but struggle to find satisfying answers, this can create an existential crisis.[5] Many of us have been blessed with intelligent inquisitive minds filled with curiosity and wonder about the world around us. Intelligence and curiosity are blessings. But they can sometimes seem like curses as well.

It has always amazed me that many do not seem to care about the big picture. They're concerned about their own day-to-day lives, their health, their careers, their finances and such. But, at least outwardly, they do not seem to spend much time thinking about the larger questions about life. Perhaps it just seems that way. Perhaps inwardly, they all ponder these deep questions, but any resulting existential crisis goes largely unexpressed or unnoticed. If so, Thoreau was probably spot on when he observed that most people live lives of quiet desperation.

There are people such as myself who *do* spend much time—perhaps, in my case, *too* much time—dwelling on what I consider to be the deeper and most meaningful questions about life. When I was in my teens or even younger, the existential questions were already growing within me. My teenage memories include many conversations with various high school friends and acquaintances. These conversations would begin unremarkably enough about this or that. Then, at some point, someone in the group would ask a deep question which would steer the conversation in a different direction. Someone might ask something like, "Do you ever wonder what life is all about?" And it would go from there. I remember this happening more than just once or twice. Often enough that someone who inserted the first deep question into the conversation was me, but not always. We all harbored

9

many questions, concerns, apprehensions, and fears about life. We just didn't share these thoughts all the time, or even acknowledged them to ourselves enough. Quiet desperation indeed.

Probably the biggest source of stress for many of us is the lack of satisfying answers that we have to these questions even today. Life can seem like a big mystery. All we really know is that here we are. We were born into a world not of our own making. We have no idea how all of this came to be. We have no idea what we're supposed to be doing here. Some of us turn to religious faith for answers that neither science nor history nor common sense can provide. But even so, the lingering questions persist.

***

Life can seem like a big test or a game. It's definitely a competition. But, if life is a game, it's one that is difficult to learn how to play, much less win. This game has clearly delineated rules we call the laws of nature, the laws of physics, civil laws and, if we choose to observe them, the laws of God. But we were not informed of these rules at the beginning of the game. We were left to figure out the rules through observation and experience. Our parents or caretakers were our first coaches in this game. Some ground rules that we learned are: (1) There are no guarantees in life, (2) we never know when something good or bad will happen, and (3) we don't know exactly how long we have in this life.

Our goal? Unclear.

It's up to us to figure out the meaning and purpose to all of this. Then, it's as if someone pushes us out onto an arena where we are expected to fight our battles and solve our problems.

A-a-a-and, ready…set…go!

Some complain that they never signed up to be part of any competition. But here we are, expected to get out there and compete for everything we need—for financial security, for housing, for clothing, for basic necessities, even for basic food needs. The biggest problem for many invariably becomes finding out how we can stem the flow of our problems so that we can just find some love, joy, and peace. Religion promises us all three. Religion doesn't necessarily provide us with love, joy, and peace. But religion *promises* us love, joy, and peace.

The Existential Crisis That Started It All

***

There's a famous line in Shakespeare's *As You Like It* which reads:

> All the world's a stage,
> And all the men and women merely Players;
> They have their exits and their entrances,
> And one man in his time plays many parts.[6]

This makes me think of a game actors play called *Prop Improv*. This is used in acting classes. Some comedians use a form of this game in their prop comedy routines. This is when an actor looks at what appears to be a random selection of props on a stage and tries to find the role called for by the props they see before them. It often feels like life works this way. We are called to figure out our roles in life based on the people, situations, circumstances, and things—the "props"—we see before us. Then we think, "Oh. Okay. I see. I'm supposed to do *this* now."

For example, if someone in real life comes across a person who is hurting and in need of immediate assistance, that person is supposed to think, "Oh, I see. My role here is to help this person right now. I'm the one who comes to the rescue. What can I do?" And then they jump into action. The person who just walks by and doesn't help can be likened to an actor who misses or ignores their cue. They would then take on the role of someone who doesn't care. But do they really want to be that person?

When you think about it, life *is* an improvisation. We have very few lines or story lines written for us in real life. Most of us don't have directors telling us how to act. We may have employers telling us how to do our jobs. Before that we had our parents/caretakers, teachers, and others telling us how to be. But how to be ourselves in our every-day lives is up to us to figure out. And, like actors on a stage, much of our lives is on full display for all of our friends and families to see.

If we just sit around and do nothing, life has a way of penalizing us for that. We don't pass our classes. We don't get paid. People start to wonder if something is wrong with us. They offer us unsolicited advice. Perhaps they recommend a good therapist. In one way or another, we are all expected to perform and be productive. All of us are merely players indeed.

***

Death. Sure, we try not to think about it. We distract ourselves by trying to think about other things. We've got television, movies, books, magazines, the internet, music, sports, all kinds of activities, conversations and other interactions with each other, and more. We distract ourselves because if we have no distractions, we can find ourselves alone with our thoughts, and that can be scary. Our thoughts might drift to the questions that deep down gnaw at us all the time.

Human beings have always had a fear of the unknown. The ultimate unknown is, of course, death. The fact is that we really don't know any more about what happens to us after we die than the cavemen did. At the root of all of our fears and anxieties is the certain knowledge that we will one day eventually die. There is no escaping it.

Research shows that fear of death is probably the underlying cause of most mental illness—stress, anxiety, depression…etc.[7] The reality is that fear of death is the primary reason that people turn to God. The Bible acknowledges this. Scripture tells us that Jesus came to "deliver them who through fear of death were all their lifetime subject to bondage." *Hebrews 2:15*. This is really sad if we think about it. Ponder this for a moment. This Scripture points out the reality that we can live our entire lives "subject to bondage" because of our fear of death. It is clear that by "fear of death," the Scripture here refers to the trauma that can result from being aware of our own mortality. This trauma was addressed in the world's first known piece of literature—*The Epic of Gilgamesh*.

Deep down, or maybe not so deep, most people are indeed enslaved by the knowledge that our eventual deaths are inevitable. We deal with our fear of death in a myriad of ways. We come up with euphemisms when we speak of death because the word death itself is too blunt or direct for many people. When someone dies, we prefer to say things like they "passed," "passed away," or "passed on." The words "deceased" or "departed" soften the bluntness too. After someone dies, they "lost their battle" or they "gave up the ghost."

We entertain ourselves with horror movies which explore the

unknown mystery of death. The recent popularity of vampires in literature and film exemplifies the curiosity about death and the afterlife.[8]

Without realizing it, we spend a great deal of our time simply avoiding death and trying to stay alive. We spend a lot of time and energy every day, most often unconsciously, taking steps to avoid death. For example, we eat when we're hungry. That sounds simple enough. But, if you think about it, we eat when we're hungry because we are ultimately afraid of starving to death. We look both ways when we cross the street because we're afraid of getting hit by a vehicle and dying from that. We seek to have good jobs with good incomes because we are afraid of being broke and dying from not being able to afford to feed ourselves. Many people diet and exercise to forestall ill health and death.

Many try to suppress the angst that results from the underlying fear of death—and other such unresolved mysteries—in negative ways such as with drugs and alcohol. Clinical depression and other mental illness can be the result of the angst. Scripture does not exaggerate when it tells us that we are subject to bondage through our fear of death. *Hebrews 2:15.* Mental illness and addiction to substances are bondage indeed.

We all have the Darwinian mandate to survive. Yet, we all know, or rather hope, that there is more to our lives than just surviving. This is where the existential crisis comes in. We've all asked ourselves at one time or another regarding our lives, "This is it?" We start out as young people with our whole lives ahead of us. It seemed like it would be a much longer journey back then. When I was in my teens, you couldn't talk to me about my future with a statement that began, "You know, by the time you're thirty…" I would think, "Thirty? That's way too far in the future for me to think about right now." But now thirty is way back in my rearview mirror. It seems like it came and went in the blink of an eye. Now, when someone brings up what might happen by the time I'm eighty, I pay attention.

Human beings seem to be the only species in this world with an awareness of our own mortality. *Ecclesiastes 9:5.* I don't think any other species in this world is cognizant of the fact that, one day without doubt, they will be dead. I know that animals have survival mechanisms in that they need to eat, and they have fight-or-flight survival skills. But do animals contemplate their own mortality the way people do? Are they aware that one day death awaits them as sure as the day they were born? Perhaps. But I think that is highly doubtful.

The average lifespan in the United States today is about 76 years.[9] Occasionally, when I bring this up in a conversation, I ask people if they know how much 76 years comes out to in days, without doing the math yet. I ask them to take a guess without actually multiplying 76 times 365 in their heads. I get guesses like a million days or more. Most people seem surprised when they realize that a 76-year lifespan comes out to only 27,740 days. I've had some people do the calculation two or three times on their calculators because they thought their calculator malfunctioned and gave them a wrong answer. That is because many people walk around with an impression that our time on this earth is *way* longer than it really is.

What is even more sobering is that if one is say, 59 years old, as I am as I write this, one has already used up a little more than 21,535 of those 27,740 days. This means that, statistically, I've got maybe a little over 6,200 days left, and that's *if* I live to the age of 76. But even if I live to be 100 years old, that's still only 36,500 days altogether. I can say this, or write this, out loud because I have come to terms with this reality.

I realize that this, as a topic of conversation, is never going to make me the life of any party. But these are truths I've always felt compelled to reckon with. Part of living in truth, I think, is coming to terms with our own mortality and being at peace with the brevity of life. The alternative is to live our lives unnecessarily anxious and stressed about a truth which we cannot change. This calls for us to apply Reinhold Niebuhr's Serenity Prayer to our lives, which says in part, "God, grant me the serenity to accept the things I cannot change, courage to change the things I can, and wisdom to know the difference."[10]

One of the most famous prayers in the world is the Hail Mary, or the *Ave Maria*, wherein every day hundreds of millions of Catholics ask our Blessed Mother to "pray for us now, and at the hour of our death." This is not being morbidly fixated on death. This is a surrendering acknowledgment of reality. There is a peace that comes from surrender to the reality that—try as we might to be in control of our lives—our lives, in reality, are not in our control and completely in the hands of God.

Little children are taught this prayer, which you may remember from your youth:

> Now I lay me down to sleep,
> I pray the Lord my soul to keep,
> If I shall die before I wake,
> I pray the Lord my soul to take. Amen.

Is it wrong to teach little children that they should say this prayer just in case they die in their sleep? This, of course, is for each parent to decide. On the one hand, the reality is that whatever control we think we have over life and death is illusory. So, it is not a bad thing to teach, even young children, that our lives are completely in God's hands, that is, our lives are really out of our control and there are no guarantees. On the other hand, we don't want the knowledge of this to cause unnecessary childhood trauma, thereby further causing the generational trauma which is the subject of this book.

Scripture tells us to be careful when we say that, today or tomorrow, we're going to do this or that. We are reminded that tomorrow is neither guaranteed nor promised. Rather than telling us to just think happy thoughts and retreat to our various happy places, Scripture encourages us to contemplate our mortality. The Bible asks us to *think*.

> For what is your life? It is even a vapour, that appeareth for a little time, and then vanisheth away. For that ye ought to say, If the Lord will, we shall live, and do this, or that.

James 4:14-15. This is not to say that we should be morbidly fixated on death and dying all the time. But I think that a healthy mature spirituality begins with an acknowledgment that, despite our best efforts, we have no more control over the day we die than we did over the day we were born. This lack of control can be maddening. Research shows that suicide attempts are really a grasp for control over when we die.[11]

Despite whatever religious beliefs we may think we have, all we really know is that we are all going through life without any idea why we're here, how we got here, or for what purpose. If you think about it, it is odd that all of this is such a mystery.

It is these existential questions that gave rise to the most widely distributed book in history—*The Holy Bible.*

***

The book in the Bible which most directly tackles existential questions is Ecclesiastes. This book explores the meaning of life by first attempting to find meaning in life if God were to be factored out of the equation. Tradition has it that Ecclesiastes was authored by King Solomon.[12] It is certainly written in the voice of Solomon. Research shows striking similarities between *Gilgamesh* and Ecclesiastes.[13]

Ecclesiastes begins by asking, "What profit hath a man of all his labour which he taketh under the sun?" *Ecclesiastes 1:3*. In other words, "What's the point of all this?" The author points out that life seems to be a pointless endless circle of recurring, boring events such as one generation dying and another generation comes, the sun rises then the sun sets, the wind blows one way then blows in the opposite direction, the rivers continually flow into the sea, yet the sea never gets full. *Ecclesiastes 1:4-7*. In his view, nothing ever happens that's new or exciting. *Ecclesiastes 1:10*. The author notes that he "was king over Israel in Jerusalem," and put all his efforts into seeking and searching out the meaning of things through his wisdom. *Ecclesiastes 1:12-13*. Yet, he could not find any reason to change his view that life is pointless. His spirit was vexed. *Ecclesiastes 1:17*. He reached the conclusion that ignorance is bliss when he said, "For in much wisdom is much grief: and he that increaseth knowledge increaseth sorrow." *Ecclesiastes 1:18*.

He tried everything. He ultimately found no lasting meaning or value in enjoying pleasure, laughing, drinking wine, pursuing wisdom, building great houses and planting vineyards and other gardens, or having great wealth and servants constantly tending to him. *Ecclesiastes 2:1-10*. He got to the point where he hated life. *Ecclesiastes 2:17*. Nothing mattered. Wise or foolish, good or evil, ultimately all meet the same fate. *Ecclesiastes 3:16-19*. He observed that human beings are really no better off than the animals in that, whether human or beast, "[a]ll go unto one place; all are of the dust, and all turn to dust again." *Ecclesiastes 3:19-20*.

The author speaks of the "wandering of the desire." *Ecclesiastes 6:9*. This refers to that constant feeling that the grass is always greener on the other side. Yet, when one gets to the other side, the grass is really the same or worse. This constant unending search for fulfillment can be the trap that St. Paul referred to as "[e]ver learning, and never able to come to the knowledge of the truth." *2 Timothy 3:7*. Life can be like that.

I remember once I walked into the library of the university in which I was enrolled at the time, with one of my professors. As we walked in, the professor told me that every time he walked into a library and looked at all those books, he became a bit disenchanted. He said that all he *really* wanted to do was quit everything and just sit and read every single book in that library. And then he said that what really made him sad was that even if he was able to do that—quit everything to just sit and read—he would not be able to read every book within his lifetime. He made me think. While being a lifelong learner is great, our goal can't be learning everything or reading everything. Forget it. That's not going to happen. We should try to focus on what is meant for us to learn. We have to prioritize.

The author of Ecclesiastes concludes that life is indeed pointless if there's no God. Ultimately, even though he observes the vanity of life throughout the book, the author refuses to accept that life has no meaning or purpose. He writes:

> Let us hear the conclusion of the whole matter: Fear God, and keep his commandments: for this is the whole duty of man. For God shall bring every work into judgment, with every secret thing, whether it be good, or whether it be evil.

Ecclesiastes 12:13-14. The author comes to the conclusion that the only meaningful thing any of us will ever do is to keep God's commandments. Whatever else we think we are going to accomplish in this life is just illusory. The sobering truth is that every single thing we do, make, build, or accomplish, will eventually come to nothing. Nothing. Every single relationship we have, positive or negative, will come to an end. If there is no God—an overarching eternal intelligent purpose to all of this—then everything there is will eventually cease to exist without any consequential impact on anything, ever. We think we're accomplishing something when, in fact, we are accomplishing nothing. The only thing worth doing is keeping God's commandments.

Jesus alluded to this when he said, "For what shall it profit a man, if he shall gain the whole world, and lose his own soul?" *Mark 8:36*. Jesus asked thought-provoking questions, and told many thought-provoking parables, which encouraged his hearers to contemplate and draw their own conclusions about life and God. Jesus never asked for anyone's unreasoning blind faith. In fact, the term *blind faith* is nowhere to be found in the Bible.

Ecclesiastes does not impose a belief in God upon anyone. It does not say, "Believe in God or else!" What it does is walk the reader through observations about life that are self-evident. The author then says that he doesn't see where any of this makes sense or can have meaning if there's no God and no eternal purpose. Making sense of life in light of death, suffering, and global injustice is difficult. He invites the reader to draw their own conclusions.

***

I know that many people reject the Bible—and faith in God altogether—precisely because they see the Bible, and faith in God, as something for ignorant and unreasoning people. I disagree. The Bible was handed down to us by people who were beginning to discover that there is much, much, more to life than had been apparent to them before. They worked hard to convey that to the people of their day. They also had the consideration and thoughtfulness to preserve their insights for future generations to tackle. Many Bible authors didn't intend to force their beliefs upon anyone. In fact, they meant for future generations to learn from their insights and take them further if they wished.

Of course, we may not see eye to eye with their worldview or their impressions of God. But they shared *their* stories. They shared *their* insights. Today, we are living *our* stories with our own insights. Today, Jesus asks us the same question he posed to St. Peter some 2,000 years ago: "Whom say ye that I am?" *Matthew 16:15*. Jesus didn't say to Peter, "You KNOW I'm the Son of God! ...RIGHT?!" No. Jesus invited Peter to draw his own conclusions. Jesus, along with all of the other people in the Bible, are reaching out to us from the past, asking us similar questions: What do *you* think of all this? What's *your* response? What say you? Do *you* have any insight to add?

I think it's sad that so many people respond by saying that they think that the Bible is just filled with worthless drivel. I like to think it's because maybe they're just not as informed as they should be about Scripture or haven't looked at it the right way. That maybe if they could see Scripture the way I do, they would love it too.

***

One of the questions that the authors of the Bible tackled is why there were clearly observable traits that seem to pass down from parent to child to grandchild and on. They noticed this without any knowledge of DNA. The Israelites in the days of Moses concluded that God punished children for the sins of their parents. They were on to something when they noticed that children often suffered the consequences, long into adulthood, for the wrongs that their parents had committed. They were right about the results, even if they may have been off about the reason.

They all deserve a lot of credit for trying to make sense of it all. Their existential crises led them to share insights, revelations, and truths that would go on to influence most of our world for thousands of years. Their work is a baton that has been passed forward through the generations. Now it is our turn to take the baton and pass it to the next generation. Let's do it.

***

One thing that all of the writings in the Bible have in common is that they all point to one God—specifically, the God of Abraham, Isaac, and Jacob. But is this the true God? Is God accurately portrayed in the Bible? If the writers of the Bible are human, and therefore fallible, how do we know that their impressions of God can be counted upon? Does the God of the Bible actually exist? Is this God false and imaginary? Can we really learn anything about a God whom the Bible itself refers to as inscrutable and unknowable? These are legitimate questions which should be explored.

CHAPTER TWO

ON THE EXISTENCE OF GOD

"I AM THAT I AM."
-- Exodus 3:14

———

DOES GOD EXIST? This is the most basic of theological questions. The only honest answer is that no one knows for sure. I do believe in the existence of God. I acknowledge, however, that my belief in God's existence is a choice that I have made based on a number of factors, none of which actually prove that God exists. I *choose* to believe in the existence of God. Further, I have chosen to believe in, and put my faith in, the God of Christianity, i.e., the God spoken of, and taught about, by Jesus Christ. But again, that is my choice. I am aware of the arguments against what I have chosen to believe. I am also aware that I cannot logically support what I have chosen to believe with anything resembling proof. But I choose to believe in it anyway.

Every day we all believe, and put our faith in, many people and things without any guarantees or proof. We put our faith in the people closest to us. We choose to believe them when they say they love us. There really can't be proof that someone loves us, nor can there be proof that we love someone else. In any relationship, we take the professions of love from the other on faith. We choose to believe them until their deeds or words move us to reconsider that belief. We expect the same faith in return.

We trust people all the time because we choose to believe that we can trust them. We trust clients or employers to pay us after we provide a service for them. We trust people when they say they're going to be there for us in various critical situations. We choose to believe and trust whom we will. Every meaningful personal relationship that we have is based entirely on belief and trust.

21

We trust the soundness of the structures around us every day without giving them much thought. We enter buildings, use elevators and escalators, use vehicles, cross bridges...etc., often without questioning the competence of those who build, inspect, and maintain these structures.

My point being that we all put our faith, hope, and trust in people and things every day without any real proof that we can trust them at all. We simply make judgment calls about others and give them the benefit of any doubt we may have until something happens that makes us feel like we can't do that anymore.

I have my reasons for putting my faith in God. I can speak about how I feel the presence of God in my heart. I can tell of how I believe that God has revealed certain things to me. I can tell how I believe that God has answered important prayers for me in my life. But the reality is that I have chosen to believe that I've experienced certain revelations from God, and that those revelations are not just my imaginings about God. I have chosen to believe that God answered some of my prayers, and that the circumstances about which I prayed didn't just pan out the way they would have whether I prayed or not. Based on my testimony, others may choose to believe in God as I do. That would be their choice to make.

We all *choose* whether to believe in God. It's really that simple. Arguments about whether God exists are pointless and almost always fruitless. A good discussion about God can be great providing that, in the end, we all respect each other's decision to choose whether to believe. It is always a choice.

Many mistakenly think that compelling someone to believe that their own impression of God is correct and that the other's impression of God is wrong is evangelism. This is incorrect. True evangelism involves empowering and freeing others to form their own edifying impressions of God, which can lead them to become their best selves.

* * *

People are either believers or nonbelievers in God. This dichotomy in its simplest form divides people into two camps: theists and atheists.

On the Existence of God

An atheist is someone who does not believe in the existence of any god. The atheist does not simply reject the god or gods of any particular religious tradition. The atheist rejects the idea that any supernatural or spiritual entity had anything to do with the creation of our universe. The atheist has concluded that there are no gods, and that there are no other supernatural spirits such as angels, demons...etc. For the atheist there is no heaven, there is no hell, there is no human soul, there is no afterlife. There is nothing other than the natural world that can be perceived empirically and observed scientifically.

A theist is someone who believes in the existence of some form of "god." This god could be the universe itself. This god is not necessarily the god of any particular religious tradition. If a theist rejects the traditional God of the Bible, this does not make them an atheist if they believe in any sort of supernatural or extra-natural intelligent force at work in the universe. As long as there is some kind of belief in any immanent or transcendent extra-natural force, that is theism.

In regard to theism and atheism, there are only four possible categories into which we all must fall.

First, there is Gnostic Atheism. A gnostic atheist is someone who claims to believe that they are 100% convinced that there is no god of any kind. A gnostic atheist does not acknowledge the possibility that God may exist.

Second, there is Agnostic Atheism. An agnostic atheist also claims to believe that there is no god of any kind, but acknowledges that they may be wrong. An agnostic atheist acknowledges the possibility that God may exist.

Third, there is Gnostic Theism. A gnostic theist is someone who claims to believe that they are 100% convinced of the existence of God. A gnostic theist does not acknowledge the possibility that God may not exist.

Fourth, there is Agnostic Theism. An agnostic theist claims to believe in the existence of God, but also acknowledges that they may be wrong. An agnostic theist acknowledges the possibility that God may not exist.

Of the four categories mentioned, I propose that we all fall into just two of them. When it comes to the existence of God, we are all agnostic, i.e., we are all either agnostic atheists or agnostic theists. No one can be 100% sure that there is no such thing as any kind of intelligent force at work in our universe. By the same token, no one can be 100% sure that God exists. Therefore, the four categories are narrowed down to two—agnostic theist and agnostic atheist.

Everyone who claims to be a gnostic theist, i.e., 100% sure of God's existence, is in reality an agnostic theist who thinks that they are a gnostic theist. I personally fall into the agnostic theist category along with everyone else who claims to believe in God.

I suppose there may be another category made up of people who sincerely do not care one way or the other whether God exists, and haven't given the matter much thought, or formed an opinion about it. However, I doubt that such people actually exist, at least not in very large numbers. How can someone really not care about something that so fundamentally goes to the heart of the very meaning of our lives and existence?

They do care. They're just not admitting it.

***

There is probably no one who believed in God and the Risen Christ more so than St. Paul of Tarsus. There is no one in the early church who did more to spread the gospel of the Risen Christ than Paul. However, he was a human being, with all of the shortcomings that go with that. Therefore, even he was not 100% certain about God's existence or that Jesus had risen from the dead. Paul too was an agnostic theist.

In a New Testament epistle to the then nascent church in first century Greece, Paul briefly entertained the possibility that his teaching on the resurrection of the dead and the resurrection of Christ might not be true. He said that "if Christ be not risen, then is our preaching vain, and your faith is also vain." *1 Corinthians 15:14*. He went on to ponder that, if Christ had not been raised from the dead, then "we are found false witnesses of God; because we have testified of God that he raised up Christ: whom he raised not up, if so be that the dead rise not." *1 Corinthians 15:15*. He concludes his thoughts on the possibility that Jesus had not been resurrected by reflecting that "[i]f in this life only we have hope in Christ, we are of all men most miserable." *1 Corinthians 15:19*.

Paul acknowledged the possibility that he might have been wrong. There is no shame in admitting that we might be wrong about what we believe. And it does not mean that our faith is disingenuous. It is always foolishness to think that we can't be wrong. Scripture teaches us that "a fool is right in his own eyes: but he that hearkeneth unto counsel is wise." *Proverbs 12:15*.

Interestingly, in his epistles, Paul never mentions the famous road to Damascus incident where the Acts of the Apostles says that he was accosted by the Risen Christ. *Acts 9:4*. In his discussion about resurrection, he did not assert that he *knew* Jesus had risen from the dead because he saw him and heard him on that day. He affirmed his *belief* in the resurrection of the dead, and the resurrection of Jesus. And left open the possibility that he might have been wrong.

***

For confirmation of what I am saying, you need only to look within yourself. If you claim to be an atheist—admit it—there's a part of you that is concerned that you might be wrong. You're not 100% sure that there's no God. That's why you keep reaffirming to yourself that there's no God, either out loud or just in your mind.

Likewise, if you are a believer in God, you probably have your doubts too. We all do. We're not 100% sure that God exists. That's why—like the atheist—many of us believers keep reaffirming our belief in God to ourselves and each other. This reaffirmation often takes the form of prayers, reading the same Scripture passages repeatedly, regular church attendance, listening to preachers tell us the same things over and over again...etc. We constantly try to reassure ourselves that we are not delusional for putting our faith, hope, and trust in God. Like King David, what many believers long for is vindication for having put our faith in God. *Psalm 7:8*.

This dynamic of reaffirmation can be observed in many churches. Rarely do preachers teach congregants something that they did not already know. Most preachers simply reaffirm what their congregants already believe or know, to which the congregants respond with an "Amen" or a least a nod of agreement. If the preacher begins to say things that the congregants don't believe or agree with, there is the underlying threat that they will find themselves a different preacher or church. So, are they really there to learn, or are they there to have their existing opinions and beliefs affirmed?

St. Paul warned Timothy, whom he had trained to be a preacher, that there would be congregants who would "not endure sound doctrine" but would seek out teachers who would tell them what their "itching ears" want to hear. *2 Timothy 4:3-4*. Unfortunately today, too many sermons and homilies are planned and given so as not to offend, put off, or challenge congregations at all. Most churches today never challenge their congregations to go beyond their comfort zones.

***

To improve our self-esteem, many of us use positive affirmations. These affirmations usually consist of positive statements about ourselves which we say over and over again until we internalize them into our subconscious minds. These positive affirmations are supposed to stop us from believing negative images of ourselves in our own minds. We're supposed to repeat these positive affirmations to ourselves precisely because we may not *really* believe the positive statements about ourselves yet.

Similarly, Christians often do positive affirmations amongst ourselves about God and how great it is to believe in God. I've wondered if the reason we do this is similar to the reasons that people with low self-esteem keep repeating positive affirmations about themselves, i.e., maybe we keep reaffirming our belief in God to ourselves and others precisely because we don't *really* believe it ourselves yet. In many groups of Christians, this kind of thing goes on all the time.

"God is good!"

"Praise Jesus!"

"Amen, sister!"

"Preach it!"

"Jesus is coming back!"

"Amen!"

You never see any group of people doing this regarding undisputed facts.

"Two plus two equals four, brother!"

"Amen to that!"

"Water is made of two parts hydrogen and one part oxygen!"

"Truth!"

There is no need to keep reaffirming undisputed facts to each other like that. That's why no one does it. However, religious people reaffirm our belief in God to ourselves and others all the time precisely because the existence of God is not an undisputed fact. Even we are not 100% convinced.

***

Atheists reaffirm their beliefs to themselves and each other too. There are countless books, magazines, websites, and organizations with meetings dedicated to the propagation of the belief that neither God nor anything supernatural exists. And, yes, the proposition that there is no Creator—or intelligent force behind the existence of our universe—is a *belief.* As is the proposition that there is an intelligent Creator behind it all. Neither is a proven fact.

One thing that atheists have going for them is that, in the age-old debate about whether God exists, the burden of proof is on the theists to prove that there is a God. Usually in debates and arguments, one does not need to prove a negative. For example, in a hypothetical debate about whether unicorns exist, the burden of proof would be on those who wish to demonstrate that unicorns are real. It would not suffice for them to simply challenge the other side to prove that there are no such things as unicorns. In the same way, the burden of proof is on believers to demonstrate that God exists.

In the United States, we have a First Amendment right to believe in God or not. Therefore, as is the case with theists, atheists have the right to express their opinions and beliefs about God. They may not see their atheism as being an opinion or belief. But it is. No one has conclusively proven that there is no God, i.e., no one has proven that there is no intelligent force or design at work behind the existence of our universe.

However, the inability to prove that something exists does not necessarily prove its nonexistence. One example of this is how Democritus and Lucretius believed that all matter was made up of atoms. The seemingly crazy theory of "atomism"[1] was ridiculed for more than 2,000 years until Einstein came along and proved the existence of atoms. Atoms always existed. But because they were undetectable to the five human senses—even using the most sophisticated available technology—people were convinced that atoms did not exist for thousands of years after some ancient Greek philosophers proposed that they do. The same might be the case with God. Today, God is undetectable to any of our five senses. This may not always be the case.

CHAPTER THREE

OUR FALSE IMAGINARY GOD WITHIN

"For if the truth of God hath more abounded through my lie unto his glory; why yet am I also judged as a sinner?"
-- Romans 3:7

———

I PERSONALLY DO believe that a perfect God exists. But I also believe that humans are incapable of grasping any meaningful understanding of God. As imperfect and flawed beings, the best we're ever going to do is have an imperfect and flawed understanding of God. We pray to and worship our own individual impressions of God. We each have our own individual human understanding of God within us. This goes as well for the people described in the Bible, and the people who wrote and compiled the Bible. All of them.

Even atheists have an impression of God. Their impression of God is the God they have chosen to reject. They have their own impression of God in their minds, as we all do, and then come to the conclusion that it doesn't make sense to believe in that God. So, the believer and the atheist have this in common: Both have their own impression of God within, which they have chosen to either accept or reject.

On the one hand, for believers, there is the one true God, the creator of everything, about whom we can really know nothing. This is the God whom Scripture says created us in his image and likeness. *Genesis 1:26.* But on the other hand, in our own individual minds and hearts is the God whom we have created for ourselves in *our* image and likeness. Unfortunately, because we are all flawed human beings, our understanding and impression of God is necessarily flawed and false. This necessarily false and flawed God within us is the God whom we worship, pray to, and obey. We're never going to have an understanding of God that even comes close to the indescribable reality.

We are all guilty, to one extent or another, of trying to shape God in our own image and likeness. This God then becomes a false imaginary God. This often becomes the God who always has the same worldview as we do. This is often the God who judges *others* harshly for doing wrong, but completely understands why *we* do wrong and overlooks our sins, or doesn't consider our wrongdoings to be sin at all. This God often rubber-stamps whatever hateful or bigoted opinions about others we may express. In short, we can control this false imaginary version of God and put words in his mouth to make him say anything we want him to say.

Worshipping this false imaginary God within us is just as wrong as worshipping false idols. A seriously distorted image of the true God is just as sinful, and potentially damaging, as the golden calf created by some Israelites while Moses was on Mount Sinai. *Exodus 32:4*. When we worship our false imaginary God within, we break the first of the Ten Commandments: "I am the LORD thy God. ... Thou shalt have no other gods before me." *Exodus 20:2-3*.

I believe that this false imaginary God within all of us has been giving the one true God a bad name for many centuries. The true God—about whom we can know nothing—gets the blame for all of the heinous acts committed in God's name by followers of their own false imaginary versions of God within themselves. All of the atrocities committed in God's name throughout history were actually perpetrated in the name of the false imaginary God within the minds of the perpetrators of the atrocities.

***

Our individual views of God are like what we see in cloud formations or inkblots from a Rorschach test. What we perceive reveals much about ourselves and our psychological makeup. What we perceive about God reveals nothing about God.

Our individual perceptions of God are the only reality of God that really matters for each of us. As human beings, we are each incapable of a completely objective and accurate understanding of God. Such a thing is impossible for us. The best we can do is decide for ourselves first, if we even believe in the existence of God at all and second, what our understanding of God entails.

In a conversation recorded in Scripture, Jesus asked his disciples, "Whom do men say that I the Son of man am?" *Matthew 16:13*. His disciples responded with various answers. Then Jesus asked his more pointed question, "But whom say *ye* that I am?" *Matthew 16:15* (emphasis added). For Christians, the operative question for each of us is: Who is *my* God? Who is *my* Jesus? Even the apostles in Jesus's day had their own individual impressions of God and Jesus within each of them.

In the days of the New Testament, there was a very serious dispute between Peter and Paul. Peter's God told him that Jesus came as the Messiah for the Jewish people. Therefore, if Gentiles wished to follow the Risen Christ, Peter ordered that they were to first convert to Judaism, which meant circumcision for men, and then they could accept Jesus as their Messiah as practicing Jews. *Galatians 2:14*. Paul's God, on the other hand, told him that it mattered not whether one was Jewish. Paul's God told him that God neither discriminated against nor favored anyone based on creed, gender, or ethnicity. This is why Paul famously wrote: "There is neither Jew nor Greek, there is neither bond nor free, there is neither male nor female: for ye are all one in Christ Jesus." *Galatians 3:28*.

This dispute between Peter and Paul became heated. Was God speaking one truth to Peter and then another truth to Paul? One would think that God would not be inconsistent like that. It is clear that Peter and Paul each *perceived* the will of God in different ways. Without Jesus around to settle the dispute, they each relied on their *own* impression of what God would have them do.

Paul wrote that when he met up with Peter, he "withstood him to the face" over this issue. *Galatians 2:11*. Catholics consider Peter to be the first pope. This means that Paul stood up to the pope, and disagreed with his impression of God. According to Paul, Peter and the other apostles recognized Paul as an apostle to the gentiles. *Galatians 2:1-10*. Paul, who was not one of the twelve apostles, and never knew Jesus before the Crucifixion, considered himself to be equal to the twelve apostles. This annoyed the Twelve. In reference to James, Peter, and John—Jesus's inner circle—Paul said they were men "who *seemed* to be pillars." *Galatians 2:9* (emphasis added). Paul begrudgingly acknowledged their authority. Paul didn't just blindly accept Peter's impressions of God, even though Peter was personally appointed leader of the church by Jesus himself. *Matthew 16:18*.

***

Using Paul as our example, we should never just blindly accept anyone else's impression of God as our own. Yes, we should definitely take the impressions of the wise and spiritually mature people whom we respect into consideration. This can include our various religious leaders, and the religious literature throughout the ages, including Scripture. But ultimately, we get to each decide for ourselves whether we believe in God, and who God is for us.

We're never going to have a perfect impression of God. The most we can hope for is a healthy impression of God as opposed to an unhealthy one. Our impression of God is linked to the health of our minds. An unhealthy mind will indubitably have an unhealthy impression of God. We can know that our impression of God is an unhealthy one if acting on our beliefs about God causes us to hurt or do harm to ourselves or others.

***

There are things about our individual impressions of God that are important to understand. I believe that most atheists reject either their own flawed impressions of God, or they adopt someone else's false imaginary impression of God, and then reject that. To that I would say that many people's impressions of God *should* be rejected.

As a believer in God, I get it. I completely understand why there are people who choose to refuse to believe in God. I'm not sanctimonious enough to pretend not to understand how someone could choose to not believe in God. After all, there is no proof at all of God's existence. And the level of suffering and injustice in this world makes a great case for atheism.

I also believe that—because the impressions of God that everyone has are necessarily flawed defective versions of God—we can actually experience trauma at the hands of our God. There are people who believe in a God that wants to send them to hell. There are people who believe in a God who is out to get them. There are children who believe in a God who decided to take away *their* mommy or daddy or other loved one, yet is good to *other* children but not them. There are people who believe that God wants to send everyone except them, and their like-minded friends, to hell. And they are fine with that.

We believers need to be more sensitive to why many people reject God altogether. We need to remember that they are actually rejecting God as God was presented to them. We need to take more responsibility for how we represent God to others. We do this through our words and deeds. Many people are rejecting God based on the conduct they perceive of those of us who claim to follow and believe in God.

Many believers share their testimony about God with others. As well-meaning as some of us can be, sometimes our version of God can be traumatizing to others. The God we present to others may be disconcerting to them. We need to acknowledge that we may be guilty of misrepresenting God or Jesus because of our insensitivity.

I was a theology teacher at a Catholic high school for some 25 years. I, therefore, contributed to the impressions of God of thousands of high school students over the years. I was always aware of the daunting nature of this task. And I hope that whatever trauma I may have passed along during that time was minimal and benign.

Throughout my years as a religious educator, I witnessed a practice among some religious leaders in which the leader would say to a group, in call-and-response fashion, "God is good!" The group responds, "All the time!" The leader then says, "All the time!" The group responds, "God is good!" On its face, this seems harmless enough. However, those who engage in this call-and-response often neglect to consider that there may be individuals in the group whose lives may be going through difficult circumstances—a serious illness, the death of a loved one, a child who just lost a parent, or any one of the many traumatic experiences too numerous to list here. Imagine sitting in such a group where you feel like God is allowing you or your loved ones to "go through hell" while everyone around you is saying how good God is to them "all the time." An individual can feel abandoned or rejected by God in this situation. That feeling of abandonment and rejection from God is actually a recurring theme in the Bible, which is one of the main issues of this book.

If we're not careful, our well-intentioned attempts to bring God's word to others can sometimes backfire. They can wind up traumatized by the very impression of God which we have helped to foster in their minds and hearts.

We all have our own childhood trauma which we inherited from people who themselves had childhood trauma before us. We're human. Passing on trauma is what we do. We can't help it. One way we can pass down trauma is by sharing our flawed and defective impressions of God with our children and others. This is one of the things that the Bible has been trying to convey to us all this time. We can only try to do better and ask God, and others, for mercy and forgiveness for those times that we fall short.

***

Regarding impressions of God, there are noticeable differences between Moses's God and, say, the God of the writing prophets of the Bible. And there are differences between the God of each of the writing prophets. This can explain why God seems to change as readers progress from the beginning to the end of the Bible. One the one hand, Scripture emphasizes that God does not change. *Numbers 23:19; Malachi 3:6.* On the other hand, God does seem to become more patient and merciful as we progress from the beginning to the end of the Bible.

Towards the beginning of the Bible, God, among other things, throws Adam and Eve out of the Garden of Eden, *Genesis 3:22-24*, killed all but eight people with a worldwide flood, *Genesis 7:23*, killed all the people in Sodom and Gomorrah, *Genesis 19:24-25*, wanted to kill Moses, *Exodus 4:24*, hardened Pharaoh's heart to make him stubbornly refuse to free the Israelites, *Exodus 7:13-14*, then killed all of the firstborn in Egypt in retaliation for Pharaoh's stubbornness, *Exodus 12:29*, and gave leprosy to Moses's sister Miriam for daring to want to share leadership with Moses, *Numbers 12:9-10*.

But in the New Testament, Jesus speaks of a loving God who punishes no one, but rather "maketh his sun to rise on the evil and on the good, and sendeth rain on the just and on the unjust." *Matthew 5:45.* In his parable of the Wheat and the Tares, Jesus teaches that good people and evil people are permitted to co-exist in this world until the judgment at the end of the world. *Matthew 13:24-30*. Jesus's God was a kinder and more loving God.

So, what happened? Did God become kinder, gentler, and more patient? No. An eternal omniscient God would not change. As the generations went by, the people in the Bible, and the Bible authors, began to perceive a kinder, gentler, and more patient God. The impression of God of the authors of the Bible progressively changed. God did not change.

Christians believe that Jesus Christ is God. *John 1:1*. Scripture tells us that "Jesus Christ is the same yesterday, and to day, and for ever." *Hebrews 13:8*. God does not change. The authors of Scripture eventually spoke of a God who is loving, patient, kind, and merciful, who was always so and never changed. They purposely supplanted the images of the angry vengeful God of the prior accounts in the Bible. They were saying that the angry, vengeful, and genocidal God was a false impression of God. *That* God never existed.

CHAPTER FOUR

THE UNKNOWABLE INSCRUTABLE GOD

"No man hath seen God at any time."
-- John 1:18

———

THE CHURCH TEACHES that when interpreting the Bible, "attention must be given to the content and unity of the whole of Scripture if the meaning of the sacred texts is to be correctly worked out."[1] The Church acknowledges that the correct meaning of Scripture passages must be deciphered. The meaning of many parts of the Bible is rarely plain and obvious. The "unity of the whole of Scripture" can be difficult to determine. There are many disparate views and portrayals of God throughout the Bible. Many of these views and portrayals of God seem to be contradictory, inconsistent, and incompatible.

John Calvin (1509-1564) asserted "that a seed of religion is divinely sown in all, scarcely one in a hundred is found who cherishes it in his heart, and not one in whom it grows to maturity."[2] Regarding knowledge of God, he went on to say that "in regard to the true knowledge of him, all are so degenerate, that in no part of the world can genuine godliness be found."[3] Calvin maintains that our fallen human nature prevents us from attaining any meaningful knowledge of God. He doesn't say specifically, but I wonder if he meant this to apply to the authors of the Bible as well. After all, the Bible was written by imperfect fallen human beings, and Calvin did say that *"all* are so degenerate."[4]

According to Calvin, the Fall affected man's image of God. Calvin's use of the term "miserable men" here refers to "the miserable ruin into which the revolt of the first man has plunged us."[5]

Mingled vanity and pride appear in this, that when

37

> miserable men do seek after God, instead of ascending higher than themselves as they ought to do, they measure him by their own carnal stupidity, and, neglecting solid inquiry, fly off to indulge their curiosity in vain speculation. Hence, they do not conceive of him in the character in which he is manifested, but imagine him to be whatever their own rashness has devised.[6]

I'm not a Calvinist, but I think he was correct here. Human beings are incapable of understanding the fulness of God. The image of God throughout the Bible is necessarily tainted by the fallen and imperfect human beings who conveyed that image. In the Bible, imperfect people portray God imperfectly.

Calvin seemed to make an exception to his rule—about all people being unable to know God—for the authors of the Bible. On the one hand, he says that Scripture "shows us the true God clearly."[7] On the other hand, he says that, in Scripture, we find a "gathering together [of] the impressions of Deity."[8] He admits that the Bible contains the impressions of God of fallen and imperfect human beings. Yet, he doesn't really explain how imperfect people can produce a clear image of God.

***

When I say that all humans have our own individual impressions of God, including the people of the Bible, I am *not* saying that God exists only in our imaginations. We have impressions of God in the same way we have impressions of all the people in our lives. We rely on our impressions of even the people closest to us. We do not know their every thought and actions. Our impressions of the people in our lives, even those closest to us, are based on our interactions with them, what we may hear about them, and our personal observations of them. We cannot get into the minds and hearts of anyone we know. We may think that we know someone well, and that may very well be the case. But each person in our lives is a person who is distinct from our impression of that person.[9]

We've all had the experience of having someone we thought we knew, say or do something that forces us to change our impression of them. The fact is that unless we are somehow able to observe every second of someone's life from birth—and observe every single experience they go through—we don't really fully *know* them. If this goes for the human beings in our lives, imagine how much less we can really know about an eternal, omniscient God.

***

Despite the fact that the obvious purpose of Scripture is to lead people to know God—laced throughout the Bible is the clear declaration that God cannot be known. God cannot be understood. *Job 26:12-14*. God's greatness is unsearchable. *Psalm 145:3; Romans 11:33-34*. God's thoughts and ways are higher than our thoughts and ways. *Isaiah 55:8-9*. The light of God is unapproachable. *1 Timothy 6:16*.

In Scripture, St. Paul said to churches in first-century Greece: "But now, after that ye have known God, or rather are known of God..." *Galatians 4:9*. Note how Paul backpedaled a little bit after he said his audience knew God. He was aware that no one can really *know* God. God is inscrutable. We are only capable of knowing "those things which are revealed" to "us and to our children forever, that we may do all the words of this law." *Deuteronomy 29:29*.

The Church teaches that the "divinely revealed realities which are contained and presented in Sacred Scripture have been committed to writing under the inspiration of the Holy Spirit."[10] In composing the sacred books, God chose writers and "made use of their powers and abilities." God acted "in them and through them." But the Church recognizes these writers of the Bible as its "true authors."[11] The Church does *not* teach that the Bible was dictated verbatim to its writers by God. The Bible is a product of imperfect flesh and blood human beings like you and I. Since the Bible was written by human beings, it is therefore not perfect. It can't be. The weak link in any divine revelation from a perfect God to imperfect human beings is, of course, the imperfect human beings.

Belief in God usually involves the belief that God is perfect. I agree that if God exists, and is whom I believe him to be, God must be perfect. But even that being the case, it still means that if God speaks through, or uses, human beings in any way, the outcome of that use will be less than perfect due to the involvement of flawed human beings.

***

The people who lived during the days in which the stories of the Bible were set, and during the days when the Bible was written, were very primitive compared to people today. Their sense of right and wrong was just beginning to develop. Their knowledge of science was virtually non-existent. Little children today know more science than the wisest sages of biblical times.

Our world today would probably have been beyond the wildest imagination of the people of the Bible. For instance, every year hundreds of millions of people today travel by jet. We get to see the earth from some 30,000 feet in the air, travelling at roughly 500 miles per hour. We get to see the clouds beneath us as we soar across the sky. The people of the Bible thought of clouds as the abode of gods and angels. That people flying above the clouds would become an everyday occurrence would surely have been unimaginable to Moses, or anyone else back then. Flying above the clouds was seen by them as a feat reserved solely for the gods. If we were able to travel back in time to the biblical days—our knowledge, skills, and technology would make us seem godlike to the people of that time.

The world of the people of the Bible, as they understood it, was a flat earth made up entirely of the ancient Near East region. *Isaiah 11:12; Revelation 7:1*. They believed that the flat earth was firmly established and did not move. *1 Chronicles 16:30; Psalm 93:1, 96:10, 104:5*. They believed that the earth existed before the sun and the other stars. *Genesis 1:14-19*. They believed that the sky—which they equated with heaven—was so close, that it could be reached with a large enough tower, *Genesis 11:4*, or ladder, *Genesis 28:12*.

***

St. Augustine of Hippo (354-430) was one of the most brilliant theological thinkers ever. However, it disturbed him that science-minded thinkers were beginning to suspect and assert that the earth is round. He was uncomfortable with this idea, which he referred to as

40

"scientific conjecture."[12] In *City of God*, he wrote:

> But as to the fable that there are Antipodes, that is to
> say, men on the opposite side of the earth, where the
> sun rises when it sets to us, men who walk with their
> feet opposite to ours, that is on no ground credible.[13]

Augustine argued that, even if it were to be "scientifically demon-strated that the world is of a round and spherical form," it did not "immediately follow that it is peopled" on its other side, and that "it is too absurd to say, that some men might have taken ship and traversed the whole wide ocean, and crossed from this side of the world to the other."[14] It concerned him that there might have been people on the other side of the world that are not mentioned or known of in the Bible. It was problematic for him because he wondered how they could have been descendants of Adam if they lived on the other side of the world, and the authors of the Bible didn't seem to know of their exist-ence. For Augustine, the existence of people on the other side of the world, living in then unknown lands, undermined his entire belief in the Bible. So, he rejected that whole idea saying, "For Scripture ... gives no false information."[15]

However, Augustine *did* have a brilliant mind. His contributions to Christian theology cannot be overestimated. Most of what he wrote is still espoused by the brightest Christian theologians of our time. Au-gustine pretty much defined Christian thought on important matters like creation, anthropology, ecclesiology, eschatology, original sin, pre-destination, epistemology, just war, free will, natural law, and sexuality. He also opined against antisemitism and slavery. But on this matter of whether the earth was round, with people living on the other side, he could not have been more wrong.

Augustine came to the wrong conclusion because he could not ac-cept that the Bible could contain erroneous or incomplete historical information. He assumed that if the authors of the Bible wrote under the inspiration of the Holy Spirit, that this was akin to God writing the Bible himself. And if God is the true author of the Bible, the Bible could therefore contain no errors, relevant omissions, or contradic-tions. In the case of the science regarding the round earth, he rejected the science in order to preserve his belief in the inerrancy of Holy

Scripture.

Augustine did not want to reckon with the fact that the Bible was written by flawed human beings just like him—and you and I—who had a corrupted and distorted image of God, as per John Calvin.

***

St. Paul is quoted in Scripture as saying that, in the past, God "winked at" what people did out of ignorance. *Acts 17:30.* Paul noticed that God's reported interactions with people in his past was different than how God seemed to interact with people in his day. That's because people's impressions of God developed and changed for the better in the 2,000 years from Abraham to Paul.

It stands to reason then that people's impressions of God would be expected to have developed and changed for the better in the 2,000 years since Paul. It is a mistake for us to view God with the same lens with which ancient peoples viewed God in the past.

If Moses were to have had the last word on God, there would not have been any need for subsequent prophets after him. But there were many. The New Testament tells us that

> God, who at sundry times and in divers manners spake in time past unto the fathers by the prophets, hath in these last days spoken unto us by his Son, whom he hath appointed heir of all things, by whom also he made the worlds.

Hebrews 1:1-2.

In regard to how each of us perceives God, St. Paul wrote that "now we see through a glass, darkly; but then face to face." *1 Corinthians 13:12.* Our individual perceptions of God are obscured, very partial, and therefore very flawed. We do the best we can to perceive God. But even our best efforts fall very, very short. Until we get to see God face to face—i.e., the beatific vision—we know next to nothing about God really. Paul went on to say, "Now I know in part; but then shall I know even as also I am known." *1 Corinthians 13:12.* This applies to St. Paul as well as to all of the other authors of the Bible. In the Bible we read their *perceptions* of God which, by St. Paul's own admission, are seen "through a glass, darkly."

***

Mother Teresa of Calcutta (1910-1997) was considered by many to be the epitome of holiness. People often used her as a modern-day example of perfect piety. It is for this reason that she was fast-tracked to canonization as a saint in the Catholic Church in 2016, just nineteen years after her death.

For almost 50 years, Mother Teresa experienced what is known as "a dark night of the soul."[16] Only Mother Teresa's spiritual directors and bishop knew about her lifelong dark night experience. Her spiritual journals became public knowledge in 2007 during her beatification cause.

In a letter to her bishop dated February 28, 1957, Mother Teresa wrote:

> There is so much contradiction in my soul. Such deep longing for God, so deep that it is painful, a suffering continual, and yet not wanted by God, repulsed, empty, no faith, no love, no zeal.[17]

It is interesting that, because God never seemed to answer her prayers, Mother Teresa felt ignored, abandoned, and rejected by God. This sense of abandonment, betrayal, and rejection from God is a recurring theme throughout Scripture. This is a grievance expressed by many of the holiest people in the Bible—right up to and including Jesus. *Matthew 27:46; Mark 15:34.*

Mother Teresa was well aware of how the general public perceived her. About one public appearance, she wrote to an adviser: "I spoke as if my very heart was in love with God—tender, personal love. If you were (there), you would have said, 'What hypocrisy.'"[18] In 1959, she wrote:

> I utter words of community prayers—and try my utmost to get out of every word the sweetness it has to give—but my prayer of union is not there any longer—I no longer pray.[19]

Mother Teresa was not a hypocrite. She was very sincere in that, despite her long "dark night of the soul," she always strove to know God and be close to God. And she was honest enough to admit to herself, and her close advisers, that she wasn't sure about God's existence. She did not feel the need to convince herself, and others close to her, that she had an unwavering 100% faith in God. This is the opposite of hypocrisy.

The fact that the general public was unaware of her struggles is understandable. She was entitled to her privacy in that regard. Everyone's relationship with God, their view of God, their personal prayer life, if any, is their personal private business.

I think Mother Teresa was too tough on herself. She felt like a hypocrite because she was a world-renowned religious leader who did not have a 100% assurance about the existence of God. She needed someone to tell her that everyone has their doubts. Somebody should have comforted her by showing her that nobody is 100% certain that God exists. Perhaps none of the bishops in which she confided were courageous enough to admit to her that, at least sometimes, they had doubts about God's existence too. Such an admission may have made her feel better. The feeling of being ignored, abandoned, and rejected by God is, in fact, a universal human experience.

I believe Mother Teresa was an example of someone who felt traumatized by her impression of God. Her God rejected her pleas for intimacy. She couldn't understand why God seemed to ignore her. She felt abandoned and rejected by God. But she had integrity in that she didn't pretend that God spoke to her. She pined for a genuine relationship with God for all of her adult life. But despite whatever misgivings she may have had about God, she lived a life of piety and service to the poorest of the poor.

The real hypocrites are the religious leaders who publicly claim to have 100% faith in God, and who claim that God speaks to them, yet secretly live their lives as if God does not exist. If they really believed in God, they would be afraid to live their lives as some of them do. They would be afraid to fleece their congregations to finance their own unholy activities and opulent lifestyles. They would be afraid to commit adultery or fornication. They would be afraid to sexually molest minors and/or protect those who do. They would be afraid to use religion as a basis for their bigoted and hate-filled views of others. But they are not.

***

Hindus are often mischaracterized as polytheists. They are said by some to worship as many as hundreds of millions of gods. This is not true.[20] The one "God" of the Hindus is Brahman, the ultimate truth or reality. Brahman is beyond the reach of human beings. No one knows anything at all about Brahman. Words do not begin to describe Brahman. Therefore, one person's opinion about Brahman is as good as the next. The hundreds of millions of gods in Hinduism are actually the individual impressions of Brahman within each Hindu believer. Some of the more well-known impressions are Brahma, Vishnu, and Shiva. I believe that the Hindu faith has a solid view of the incomprehensibility and inscrutability of the unknowable God.

My brief explanation doesn't begin to do justice to this 5,000-year-old religion, the most ancient on the planet. But my point is that all people can benefit from understanding—as Hindus seem to—that the most each of us can do is try our best to comprehend the incomprehensible God, and respect each other's efforts to do so as well.

If more people understood that we each have our own individual impressions of God within us, and that there is nothing wrong with that, people would realize how ridiculous it is to argue about who's version of God is correct or more accurate. The problem is that far too many people don't believe that they've formed an impression of God that is subjective and unique to them. They believe that they have an objective view of God. Their idea of evangelization is to try to persuade others to adopt their impression of God as objective truth about God. If others have different impressions of God than they do, they just consider them to be mistaken.

***

The Jesus of the Gospels shared his impressions of God with others and simply invited them to draw their own conclusions. Jesus's primary teaching tool was parables. *Matthew 13:34.* Many of his parables analogized the kingdom of heaven to something his audience understood.

Jesus taught that the kingdom of heaven is like seeds being planted, *Matthew 13:1-23*, wheat among tares, *Matthew 13:24-30*, a mustard seed, *Matthew 13:31-32*, a hidden treasure, *Matthew 13:44*, a pearl of great price, *Matthew 13:45-46*, a net that catches fish, *Matthew 13:47-50*, and a wedding feast, *Matthew 22:1-14*. Jesus taught that God is like a shepherd looking for his lost sheep, *Matthew 18:10-14*, a woman who searches her whole house for a lost coin, *Luke 15:8-10*, and a father who throws a party when his wayward son comes home, *Luke 15:11-32*.

The analogies to the kingdom of heaven and God used by Jesus in his parables were great and very inspiring. But even these analogies fall short. This is why Jesus had to use more than one. No single analogy would suffice. Jesus simply wanted to convey that God loves us and actively seeks to be in relationship with us.

Jesus's impression of God has connected with billions of people over two millennia. But it is still an impression of God. Jesus offers us his impression of God for us to accept or reject.

I believe that the teachings of Jesus are meant, in large part, to enable us to break free from the bondage that can result from having an unhealthy impression of God—that false God within us all. In Scripture, St. Paul says that God "hath reconciled us to himself by Jesus Christ, and hath given to us the ministry of reconciliation." *2 Corinthians 5:18*. Paul acknowledged the traumatic relationship between humans and God, and how the purpose of the church is to foster reconciliation between God and his people through Christ.

***

Scripture tells us that we cannot know or understand God in a cognitive way. That is not possible. Jesus tells us that we can know God because God dwells in us. *John 14:17*. Scripture also tells us that we can show that we know God by loving one another. *1 John 4:7*. Living a godly life is how we show we know God. But Scripture doesn't contemplate people knowing God in a cognitive way. Human beings are not capable of that. We are all essentially on a need-to-know basis. When it comes to God, we are called to know just enough to be able to follow God's commandments.

The Unknowable Inscrutable God

***

Ultimately, we are asked to have *faith* in God precisely because we are incapable of understanding anything about God at all. Scripture says that Moses once asked God to show him his glory. God responded by saying that no one can see his face and live. *Exodus 33:18,20.* It's not that God is hiding from us just to seem mysterious. It's that our five senses are incapable of experiencing the presence of God in his fulness. If we were to all of a sudden see God's "face,"—i.e., God in his fulness—we would likely die of shock and sensory overload. People *can* die of shock from seeing or experiencing all kinds of things.[21]

Experiencing too much truth or too much reality all at once can indeed be fatal. While we can try to imagine "heaven" and the eternal life that God has in store for us, Scripture tells us that whatever God has in store for us hasn't even entered our imaginations. St. Paul reminded Christians in ancient Greece that "it is written, Eye hath not seen, nor ear heard, neither have entered into the heart of man, the things which God hath prepared for them that love him." *1 Corinthians 2:9.* And we can all imagine some really great things!

This makes sense to me. If we think about it, it is the height of hubris and arrogance for us to believe that we human beings can know or grasp anything meaningful about an eternal, omniscient, omnipotent, and omnipresent Supreme Being. Human thought and language cannot begin to do such a God justice. There is nothing that we can say about God that even begins to describe him accurately.

For instance, we say that God is good. On a different occasion we might note that we like ice cream, and that ice cream is good. If we do, we'd be using the same adjective to describe both ice cream and God. Our words would diminish God down to the level of ice cream.

All words about God diminish God in this way, and that includes the words in the Bible. Yet, the Bible contains upwards of three quarters of a million words, almost all of which describe God or something that God allegedly said or did. In order to exchange ideas about God, we must use our words and say something. But we should be mindful to interpret what is said about God with the understanding that no words are adequate when it comes to God.

***

The biggest schism in Church history occurred in 1054 A.D. when the Catholic Church split in two resulting in the Roman Catholic Church in western Europe, and the Greek Orthodox Church in eastern Europe. As a Roman Catholic, I'm supposed to argue that the Roman Catholic Church is the true Church and that the Greek Orthodox Church left us. But the truth is that both sides of this split can trace their origins all the way back to Jesus and the Apostles. The one true Church split in two. Both sides are equally right, or wrong, as the case may be.

This schism seems to have occurred largely because of semantics. Both sides quibbled over how to exactly word their beliefs about God. It is jaw dropping how much damage the disagreement about the precise wording of beliefs about God caused the Church, in light of the fact that there are no words that can do God justice.

One of the reasons for the 1054 A.D. schism in the Church is the filiolique controversy.[22] This was a disagreement over whether the Holy Spirit proceeds from the Father and the Son, or just from the Father. It is unclear to most what that even means. But in the west, the Roman Catholic Church adopted as dogma that the Holy Spirit proceeds from the Father and the Son. In the east, the Eastern Orthodox Church adopted as dogma that the Holy Spirit proceeds from the Father only.

The Nicene-Constantinopolitan Creed (the Profession of Faith) is recited during Sunday Mass in both Roman Catholic and Eastern Orthodox churches. The Roman Catholic version of the Creed states "[a]nd I believe in the Holy Spirit, the Lord, and giver of Life, Who proceeds from the Father and the Son." In the Eastern Orthodox Church, the same faith statement ends with "[w]ho proceeds from the Father."

This controversy is particularly sad because both sides believe in the divinity of Christ, and both sides believe in the Holy Trinity, and that the Trinity is a mystery which no one can understand. Yet, both sides have parsed words over a mystery that cannot be adequately described with words, and used that as one of the pretexts for dividing the church in two.

The difference between both views is that on the Roman Catholic side, there seems to be a pecking order in the Trinity. The Son is subordinate to the Father and then the Holy Spirit is subordinate to both the Father and the Son. On the Eastern Orthodox side, the Son and the Holy Spirit seem to be equals who are both subordinate to the Father. But yet, if the Father is God, and Jesus is God, and the Holy Spirit is God, doesn't that mean that all three Persons are God and therefore equal? To say that one Person in the Trinity "proceeds" from the other makes it seem as if the Persons who proceeded from the other are created by the Person from whom they proceeded. But then they wouldn't be God at all but rather created beings.

I know, this is all very confusing. But this is what happens when people try to describe the indescribable.

***

I suppose, though, that if people are going to contemplate God and whether God exists, or share their beliefs about him, then we must say *something* about God. Speaking about an unknowable and inscrutable God is fine as long as we remember one thing: *All words are symbols.* The word *love* symbolizes our concept of love, the word *God* symbolizes our concept of God...and so on.

The best we can do is try to compare the unknowable God to something we *do* know. We compare God to a king. We compare God to a father. When Christians call Jesus the only "Son" of God, that is an analogy too. What we mean is that we believe that there was a closeness between Jesus and God that we can't explain in any better way. But *all* analogies to God fall short. Scripture asks us, "To whom then will ye liken God? or what likeness will ye compare unto him?" *Isaiah 40:18.*

The incongruity of attempting to speak about and discuss an unknowable and indescribable God has long been acknowledged by religious thinkers.[23] Apophatic theology (also known as negative theology) is an approach that describes God by negation, i.e., speaking of God in terms of what he is *not* rather than presuming to describe what God *is.* The idea being that words can accurately describe what God is not, but words will always fail to describe what God is.

An example of an apophatic statement is that God was not created. This is what the Bible and the Church teach. God has no beginning and will have no end. *Psalm 90:2.* Try to wrap your head around that one. I bet you can't. Our minds find it difficult to contemplate eternity.

Take a moment to try to contemplate a God who was *never* created—a self-existent God. Contemplate a God who was always there. Always. This raises some interesting questions. Can your mind grasp this? I don't think so. The whole premise behind the Christian doctrine of the Incarnation—the belief that God became human in Jesus—is that God revealed himself to us in a form that humans can grasp and understand because God, in his fulness, is incomprehensible to humans.

St. Paul told a story about a time when he had a mystical experience in which he had a revelation of "the third heaven." *2 Corinthians 12:2.* He referred to himself in the third person, but it is clear that he was speaking of himself. He said that "he was caught up into paradise, and heard unspeakable words, which it is not lawful for a man to utter." *2 Corinthians 12:4.* He had nothing more to say about that experience. This man wrote extensive letters to churches all around the Mediterranean region about Christ and God. Yet, when he got a glimpse of heaven in a revelation from God, he could not find the words to describe what he saw. He could not describe the indescribable.

***

If you've ever tried to do a deep dive into the mysteries of God, you know how inconclusive that always turns out to be. There are too many unanswerable questions. God is eternal, i.e., God has no beginning and no end. No one created God. God was always there.

Was there ever a time when God did not exist? Try contemplating *that.*

Try imagining nothingness. No creation, no universe, no heaven, no angels, no saints, no God—just nothing, nothing at all. I bet you can't do that either. How can there have ever been a time when there was nothing? Something cannot come from nothing. Or so we think. We know that our universe exists now. Our universe could not have come from nothing. Therefore, there must always have been something. Something must have always existed.[24]

Try to contemplate God existing alone without creating anything. This is hard to imagine as well. Was there ever a time when only God existed? No creation—just God? This would mean that God existed for some immeasurable amount of time way back when and then, at some point, for some reason, decided to create something other than himself. A good question would be, "Why?" What would motivate God to create something after not having created anything for some time prior to that?

As fun as it might be to ponder all of this, no conclusions are going to be reached. This is what Scripture means when it says that God is inscrutable. *Romans 11:33.*

***

So, if God is so unknowable and inscrutable—and there are so many divergent impressions of God offered throughout the Bible—how do we form an impression of God that is righteous, just, and loving to everyone? Are we supposed to just discard the Bible? How can we know that our impressions of God are accurate, or at least on the right track? To what extent *can* we discern the will of God?

The Bible itself provides us with the way to do this. We need to put on our Genesis 18 Abraham.

Abraham Sees Sodom in Flames
James Tissot (1836-1902)

CHAPTER FIVE

PUTTING ON OUR GENESIS 18 ABRAHAM

"He that is spiritual judgeth all things, yet he himself is judged of no man."
-- 1 Corinthians 2:15.

––––––

THE FIRST IMPRESSIONS of God in the Bible came primarily from two men—Abraham and Moses. This is the Abrahamic/Mosaic God described throughout the first five books of Moses—also known as the Torah, or the Pentateuch. Tradition has it that Moses himself wrote the Torah. If so, then yes, the impressions of the Abrahamic/Mosaic God in the Bible are primarily those of Abraham as filtered through the writings of Moses.

The Abrahamic/Mosaic God instilled fear in people by flooding the whole world, inflicting plagues, suborning genocide, and otherwise expressing his anger. In fact, the Bible tells us that Moses reluctantly did what his God wanted him to do because Moses was afraid of making him angry. *Exodus 4:14.* At one point, the Abrahamic/Mosaic God sought to kill Moses. *Exodus 4:24.* The Abrahamic/Mosaic God explicitly said that he wanted people to fear him. *Deuteronomy 10:12.* For better or worse, the Abrahamic/Mosaic God would set the template for how God is perceived by many people, even today. Whenever I refer to God as found in the first five books of Moses, I refer to the Abrahamic/Mosaic God.

In Genesis 18, when God told Abraham that he intended to destroy Sodom and Gomorrah, Abraham interceded on behalf of these towns. *Genesis 18:16-32.* Abraham challenged God to be fair and merciful rather than to just indiscriminately "destroy the righteous with the wicked." *Genesis 18:23.* At one point Abraham asks God a pivotal question, "Shall not the Judge of all the earth do right?" *Genesis 18:25.*

Challenging God to his face was something Abraham did not take lightly, nor should he have. But, did Abraham actually challenge God—as a literal reading of the biblical text conveys—or, did Abraham challenge his own *impression* of God? That is, was Abraham struggling with, and working out, his own idea of God? Abraham may have been internally asking himself, "Do I believe in a God that would indiscriminately punish the innocent along with the guilty? That wouldn't be right." Abraham used his *own* conscience to make an assessment about the righteousness of God.

I believe it would be a good thing if we all try to get in touch with our own inner Genesis 18 Abraham, i.e., our own conscience with regard to our belief in God. Our Genesis 18 Abraham would give us the courage to evaluate what we believe and have been taught about God. None of us should ever just blindly accept someone else's impression of God as our own, no matter who that person is. First, because it is mentally and spiritually unhealthy to do so. Second, because this is how dangerous cults are formed—by followers blindly accepting what a cult leader says, even if it doesn't sit well with their own consciences. The term "drinking the Kool-Aid" stemmed from a famous incident where a cult leader told his followers to commit suicide by drinking a poisoned soft drink, which most of them obediently did.[1] Their inner Genesis 18 Abraham, if permitted to speak, would have said, "Wait. This can't be right." In Genesis 18, Abraham relied on his own conscience. We all have God-given consciences, just like Abraham did.

Anyone who tries to discourage you from using your own conscience to form your *own* impression of God for yourself—and instead wants you to blindly accept *their* impression of God—is just trying to control you. They want to be a Svengali in your life. Don't let them do it. Think for yourself. Come to your own conclusions. Don't just believe whatever you're taught.

There is a largely undiscussed teaching about conscience within the doctrines of the Roman Catholic Church. It is a freeing and liberating teaching nestled right there within the pages of the official Vatican-approved *Catechism of the Catholic Church* like a proverbial Easter egg. The Catholic Church teaches that

> Man has the right to act in conscience and in freedom
> so as personally to make moral decisions. He must not

be forced to act contrary to his conscience. Nor must
he be prevented from acting according to his conscience, especially in religious matters.[2]

The Church teaching is that "[a] human being must always obey the
certain judgment of his conscience."[3] What this means is that, Catholic
teaching notwithstanding, if your mature and soundly developed conscience is at odds with what the Church teaches on any matter, the
Church says, "Follow your conscience."[4]

For Catholics, following one's own conscience when it is at odds
with Church teaching is not to be taken lightly. Church teaching per-
mits this assuming that one's conscience is mature and fully formed.[5]
Catholics must take what the Church teaches into consideration and
be fully informed about what it teaches and why. We must also be
careful not to rationalize by convincing ourselves into doing something
that, deep down, we know is wrong. But, if after careful consideration
we still believe that our own conscience is right, then we must follow
our conscience. This is not to say that we are therefore objectively in
the right. We might still be doing the wrong thing. But if we are wrong,
we would be doing the wrong thing in good conscience. It would be a
bona fide attempt to do what is right. According to Catholic teaching,
nothing we do in good conscience is imputed to us as sin.

The Church teaches that, in order for someone to be guilty of serious sin—i.e., mortal sin—the sin must be "grave matter" and committed with "full knowledge" and "deliberate consent."[6] Grave matter
means a serious violation of one of the Ten Commandments. Full
knowledge means an understanding that one is committing a grievous
act which offends God, moral standards, and natural law. Deliberate
consent means that one makes a free choice to commit an act. But if
your fully formed conscience tells you that you are in the right, the
Church teaches that you must follow your conscience.

This is the primary reason I remain in the Catholic Church, despite
all of its flaws. Catholic teaching respects my right to think for myself,
like Genesis 18 Abraham. I respect that.

***

Prophets in the Bible used their consciences to form their own impressions of God. They all reevaluated the impressions of prior prophets and offered their own perceptions of God as a substitute for the prior prophets' images of God. An example of this is how the prophet Elijah upgraded the impression of God provided by Moses.

Moses's God was made manifest on a mountain, *Exodus 3:1-6*, in strong wind, *Exodus 10:13,19; 14:21; 15:10,* an earthquake, *Numbers 16:28-34*, and in fire, *Exodus 3:2; 9:23-24; 13:21-22; 40:38*. Some 500 years after Moses, the prophet Elijah is said to have once searched for God at the top of a mountain, a strong wind, an earthquake, and then a fire. But God wasn't in any of those things. Elijah found his God instead in "a still small voice." *1 Kings 19:11-13*. Elijah opted for his *own* impression of God rather than the one provided by the accounts of Moses. It is not by accident that Elijah is said to have searched for God on a mountain, a strong wind, an earthquake, and a fire. These are all ways that Moses's God manifested himself. Elijah was specifically upgrading Moses's impression of God. Elijah's impression of God is closer to the impression of God that Jesus would eventually provide.

You might say, "Well, I'm no Elijah. Who am I to form my own impression of God?" True, you are not Elijah. This goes for all of us. But ultimately, each of us has the right to go by the impression of God that our own consciences form for us. We are not biblical prophets, and we don't need to convince others that our impressions of God are correct. Our impressions of God are personal and just for us.

There are many troubling images of God presented in the Bible. What we should do with these stories is put on our Genesis 18 Abraham, and ask if the God in the story is the God in whom we believe.

***

Tradition has it that Moses is the author of the first five books of the Bible. These books are known alternately as the Torah, the Pentateuch, and the Five Books of Moses. Modern Bible scholars believe that these books are actually a compilation of the writings of many authors. However, if the incidents described in this chapter are Moses's own accounts, or are at least based on genuine Mosaic tradition, they reveal much about the nature of Moses's relationship with God, his impression of God, and his psychological makeup.

Let's assume, for the purposes of this book, that Moses was indeed the author of these five books. On the one hand, then, Moses claimed to have a close relationship with God. He wrote that God spoke with him "face to face" the way a man speaks with a friend. *Exodus 33:11.* On the other hand, Moses didn't really trust God all that much. He seemed to have an impression of God that traumatized him at times.

***

At one point, God wanted to kill Moses. *Exodus 4:24.* This was Moses's impression of God. Moses's wife, Zipporah, concluded that God wanted to kill Moses because he had failed to have their firstborn son circumcised. *Exodus 2:22.* So, Zipporah circumcised him. *Exodus 4:25.* Right here, if I put on my Genesis 18 Abraham, I ask myself, "Is this the God I believe in? I believe in this God who wanted to kill someone because they neglected to circumcise their child?" I can't imagine that God was thinking, "Look at this guy. I call him to be my prophet, and he doesn't even circumcise his son for me. That's it, at first opportunity, I'm killing him."

Is this *your* God?

***

In his first encounter with Moses, God called him to go to the Egyptian Pharaoh and demand the freedom of the enslaved Israelites. *Exodus 3:10.* At first, Moses wanted nothing to do with this mission. He made up excuse after excuse as to why God should pick someone else. Finally, Moses relented and agreed to do it. Why? Because "the anger of the LORD was kindled against Moses." *Exodus 4:14.* Moses agreed to help free the Israelites because he sensed that God was growing angry at his reluctance. At that point, a frightened Moses was concerned for his own safety. He was afraid of his own impression of God. He obeyed God out of fear and terror.

Moses perceived God as wanting to kill him for not circumcising his son because, in Moses's view, God did a *lot* of killing. One of God's first acts, according to Moses's books, was to kill the entire human race with a worldwide flood, except for Noah, his family, and the animals on his ark. *Genesis 7:21.* That's a lot of dead people and animals. This flood story set an ominous tone. The people were admonished to live in fear of the destructive power of Moses's God. *Deuteronomy 4:3-4,10.*

The idea that God "sought to kill" Moses seems bizarre. *Exodus 4:24.* Why would God need to *seek* to kill someone? One would think that if God wanted someone dead, they would just die. Imagine walking around afraid and looking over your shoulder because you suspect that someone is out to kill you—and that someone turns out to be God?

There is research which suggests that Moses may have suffered from Religious OCD.[7] Religious OCD is motivated not so much by faith but, rather, anxiety. Those with religious OCD "might be obsessed with the idea that God is mad at them or that the devil is motivating their actions."[8] This is clearly not a healthy way to perceive God.

***

By Moses's account, God killed all of the firstborn sons throughout the land of Egypt. *Exodus 12:29.* God did this as punishment for the Pharaoh's stubborn refusal to free the Israelite slaves. Yet, Moses also repeatedly wrote that God hardened Pharaoh's heart. *Exodus 7:13; 9:12; 10:1; 10:20; 10:27; 11:10; 14:8.* Moses perceived God as thwarting his efforts to free the Israelite slaves—which God told him to do—by intentionally making Pharaoh obstinate.

God kills all of the firstborn sons in Egypt as punishment for Pharaoh's stubbornness even though God hardened Pharaoh's heart and *made* him stubborn. Genesis 18 Abraham would ask, "Is this right? Would the true God kill all of those firstborn sons in Egypt, punishing all of those families so tragically because of the stubbornness of Pharaoh, whose heart was hardened by God? ...Not fair, God."

Moses's account of what God did to Pharaoh raises a moral, ethical, theological, and philosophical quandary. Was it fair of God to hold Pharaoh responsible for being so obstinate if God himself hardened Pharaoh's heart? Did God simply use Pharaoh as a means to an end, thereby denying him his free will and devaluating his humanity? Moses's God told Pharaoh that "in very deed for this cause have I raised thee up, for to shew in thee my power; and that my name may be declared throughout all the earth." *Exodus 9:16.* God is actually quoted as saying that he raised up Pharaoh, and presumably also hardened his heart, so that he could punish Pharaoh and all the Egyptians for his hardened heart, thereby showing everyone the extent of his destructive power.

In the first century A.D., St. Paul of Tarsus briefly wrestled with this thorny issue regarding the Pharaoh in his biblical letter to the church in Rome. In a moment of candor, Paul acknowledged that some of the things that God said or did in Scripture did seem arbitrary and capricious to him. Paul addresses God's apparent arbitrariness and capriciousness with regard to the Pharaoh. In regard to Pharaoh, Paul said, "Therefore hath he mercy on whom he will have mercy, and whom he will he hardeneth." *Romans 9:18*. Paul refused to delve into the question of how God could punish someone for having a hard heart if God himself hardened that heart. He expresses no thoughts on this issue, and he discourages others from thinking about it as well. Paul wrote:

> Thou wilt say then unto me, Why doth he yet find fault? For who hath resisted his will? Nay but, O man, who art thou that repliest against God? Shall the thing formed say to him that formed it, Why hast thou made me thus?

Romans 9:19-20. Paul's answer here is simply that God can do what he wants, whenever he wants, even if it doesn't seem right.

Paul's response is similar to that of a child in a family wherein the parents are doing something the child thinks is wrong, but the child is afraid to ask the parents about it. Such a child may fear being punished for saying to their parent that they question whether they are doing the right thing. So, the child keeps their questions to themself.

It is interesting that, despite referencing the patriarch Abraham extensively in his letter to the church in Rome, he doesn't hearken back to the Genesis 18 Abraham who asked God, "Shall not the Judge of all the earth do right?" *Genesis 18:25*. Abraham teaches us that questioning the righteousness of God, or rather the righteousness of our *impression* of the unknowable God, is okay. We're allowed to do that. In doing so, we are really questioning our own sense of righteousness and justice. With Abraham, we can ask ourselves from time to time: "Do I believe in a God who is fair and just with everyone?"

ORIGINAL TRAUMA

***

We can tell if we're traumatized by our own impression of God if we find ourselves afraid to even *think* of questioning if our impression of God is right and just. If we find ourselves having thoughts which question God, or question the existence of God, and then we quickly suppress those thoughts and try to think of something else—perhaps before God finds out about those thoughts—we show that we are afraid of being punished by God for using our minds to think. This begs the question: Do we believe in a God who punishes people for thinking?

There was an episode of *The Twilight Zone* television series entitled *It's a Good Life*.[9] In this episode, a six-year-old boy possessed the power to punish people at will using just his mind. He was able to make things and people appear and disappear. He could read everyone's minds. He punished anyone who wasn't thinking happy thoughts and positive thoughts about him. Therefore, everyone was terrified of him, and constantly smiled at him, and told him that he was "a good boy."

He had the power to isolate the small town in which he, his parents, and several other adults lived. No one could leave the town. In short, the boy had godlike power over the adults in the town, and wielded it like the capricious child that he was. No matter what heinous thing the boy did—whether it was killing someone and making them disappear, or creating some three-headed animal at will—everyone placated and humored him by saying something like, "That's real fine that you've done that. That's real fine. You're a good boy. We all love you. We sure do love you."

It often seems as if people fear their impression of God and treat God the way that those people treated the boy in that *The Twilight Zone* episode.

"That's real fine that you killed all those people in that worldwide flood."

"All those firstborn sons in Egypt deserved to die. That was real fine."

"That was fine what you did to Sodom and Gomorrah."

People are often too terrified to ask, along with Genesis 18 Abraham, "Shall not the Judge of all the earth do right?" *Genesis 18:25*. Just as the people in *The Twilight Zone* episode were traumatized by that little boy, many people walk around traumatized by their own impression of God—a God of their own making.

***

What was a man to do, in Moses's day, if he suspected his wife of infidelity, yet was unable to prove it? Well, Moses's God provided the solution. Moses's God said that, if a man brought his wife before a priest accusing her of adultery without proof, the priest should administer the bitter water test. *Numbers 5:11-31*. God said that "the priest shall take holy water in an earthen vessel; and of the dust that is in the floor of the tabernacle the priest shall take, and put it into the water." *Numbers 5:17*. The priest was to give the woman contaminated water to drink—"bitter water that causeth the curse." *Numbers 5:24*.

The test was fairly simple. If the woman was innocent of committing adultery, then nothing bad would happen to her after drinking the contaminated bitter water. However, if she was guilty as charged, then "the water that causeth the curse shall enter into her, and become bitter, and her belly shall swell, and her thigh shall rot: and the woman shall be a curse among her people." *Numbers 5:27*. It has been suggested that the word thigh here is a euphemism for the woman's reproductive organs and that the belly swelling refers to a prolapsed uterus.

According to Scripture, this bitter water test procedure was permissible under "the law of jealousies." *Numbers 5:29*.

My inner Genesis 18 Abraham doesn't think that God would be okay with letting a priest make a woman suspected of adultery drink contaminated water in a test of her honesty, and then making her reproductive organs rot as punishment for lying about being unfaithful. Do I believe that an omniscient, benevolent God came up with the bitter water test? I do not.

That the biblical account is just an author's *impression* of God is demonstrated by the fact that, in it, God appears to be just as ignorant of science as the author(s) who wrote this story.

***

During the days when the Israelites were wandering in the wilderness,

the people spake against God, and against Moses,

> Wherefore have ye brought us up out of Egypt to die in the wilderness? for there is no bread, neither is there any water; and our soul loatheth this light bread.

Numbers 21:5. God apparently got all angry about the people's moaning and complaining, so he thought, "Oh, yeah? I'll teach you to talk smack about me and Moses!" So then "the LORD sent fiery serpents among the people, and they bit the people; and much people of Israel died." *Numbers 21:6*. (Again with the killing.) So the people told Moses they were sorry. They asked Moses to ask God to call off the serpents. *Numbers 21:7*.

Then, the same God who had previously told his people, as part of the Ten Commandments,

> Thou shalt not make unto thee any graven image, or any likeness of any thing that is in heaven above, or that is in the earth beneath, or that is in the water under the earth,

Exodus 20:4, told Moses to make a graven image of a serpent and set it on a pole, *Numbers 21:8*, saying "every one that is bitten, when he looketh upon it, shall live." The serpent on the pole became a source of healing for the people of Israel, which is odd in light of the account of the serpent in the Garden of Eden.

Now here's an interesting twist. Some 500 years after this incident of the serpent on the pole, King Hezekiah began his reign over Judah. *2 Kings 18:2*. According to Scripture, "he did that which was right in the sight of the LORD." *2 Kings 18:3*. Hezekiah decided to clean house by destroying all of the illicit graven images that the people had accumulated over the years. In the process, he smashed the bronze serpent which Moses had made, because up until that time the Israelites were burning incense to it. *2 Kings 18:4*. But, the Scripture—of which Hezekiah must have been aware—said that God told Moses to make the bronze serpent. *Numbers 21:18*. So, Hezekiah destroyed a graven image that Moses made himself at the behest of God, because it was a sinful graven image. See the inconsistency? Hezekiah's impression of God clashed with Moses's.

Why was Hezekiah seemingly brazen enough to destroy the bronze serpent which was made by Moses himself—at God's behest—according to Scripture? Because Hezekiah put on his Genesis 18 Abraham and used his *own* conscience. *He* made the call. He was aware of the five books of Moses, a.k.a., the Torah.[10] But he also knew that the Scriptures contain other people's *impressions* of God, and nothing more. Otherwise, he would not have dared to destroy something that Moses himself had made like that.

Hezekiah used his own conscience, and thought, "Nope. This bronze serpent is a graven image afoul of the Ten Commandments. It's got to go!" Are you seeing this? Hezekiah did not believe that the bronze serpent was of God, despite what the Scriptures say.

$$***$$

Beyond the books of Moses, we have this.

God sent two bears to maul forty-two "little children" to death, simply for making fun of a prophet for being bald. *2 Kings 2:23-24*. I know that making fun of anyone is rude and uncalled for. Yes, the little children were wrong for making fun of the man. But they were just children being children. A simple reprimand would have sufficed.

Personally, there's no way that I can accept the idea that an all-knowing, all-powerful, loving God would even contemplate sending bears to maul children to death simply because those children were teasing a man for being bald. My inner Genesis 18 Abraham certainly questions this impression of God.

Why is the story of the bears mauling children in the Bible if it portrays God as being so harsh to these children? In the time when this story was first told, it must have made sense to the people that heard it or read it. It was intended to instill respect for God—or fear of God. Disrespecting a prophet of God was the same as disrespecting God. Anyone who did so was to be punished, sometimes to the point of death. This apparently applied to little children as well.

Regarding interpreting stories like this in the Bible, the Church teaches that

> for the correct understanding of what the sacred au-
> thor wanted to assert, due attention must be paid to the

customary and characteristic styles of feeling, speaking and narrating which prevailed at the time of the sacred writer.[11]

It is important to try to understand the mindset of the people who wrote all of the Bible stories. For their own reasons, which we may not understand, the people who handed down the story of the bears mauling the children honestly believed that the story reflected positively on God.

I would say, though, that this story is a traumatizing one on its face. What say *you*? Is this story compatible with *your* impression of God? Do *you* believe that the God to whom you pray did this to those children? Should this story be taught to children? These questions are for each of us to answer for ourselves according to our own individual God-given consciences—our Genesis 18 Abraham.

***

Every year during the Christmas season, Christians all over the world celebrate the birth of Jesus. The actual birth date of Jesus is not known. But, very early on in church history, December 25 was selected as the date of Jesus's birth.[12] January 7 for Orthodox Christians.

Part of the Christmas festivities is the Visit of the Magi. *Matthew 2:1-11*. Children all over the world perform in Christmas pageants at their churches or religious schools, reenacting the visit of the three kings bearing gifts for the child Jesus. However, there is a part of this story that is never part of the holiday traditions. I speak of the Slaughter of the Innocents. *Matthew 2:12-23*. This happened right after the Visit of the Magi.

As the story goes, when the Magi arrived in Jerusalem after following the star of Bethlehem, they asked King Herod, "Where is he that is born king of the Jews? for we have seen his star in the east, and are come to worship him." *Matthew 2:2*. The magi told Herod that the birth of the king of the Jews had been predicted by prophecy. *Matthew 2:5-6*. Herod was troubled by this because he considered himself to be the king of the Jews. Herod felt threatened by what the Magi told him. He did not know the child Jesus or his family. He couldn't determine the identity of Jesus from the magi because after visiting Jesus, the magi were "warned of God in a dream that they should not return to Herod" so "they departed into their own country another way." *Matthew 2:12.* Herod initially wanted to kill the child in question in an attempt to prevent the prophecy referred to by the magi from coming true, i.e., that a recently born baby boy was destined to become the king of the Jews. Since Herod could not determine the identity of the baby who would go on to fulfill the prophecy of which the magi spoke, he

> sent forth, and slew all the children that were in Beth-
> lehem, and in all the coasts thereof, from two years old
> and under, according to the time which he had dili-
> gently inquired of the wise men.

Matthew 2:16. This was probably hundreds of children.

An angel of the Lord appeared to Joseph and told him to take the child Jesus and Mary to Egypt until further notice because Herod would try to kill Jesus. *Matthew 2:13.* It should be noted that nothing was done to warn the parents of all of those other children about Herod's intentions.

The Feast of the Holy Innocents is observed by the Catholic Church every December 28.[13] It is played down and rarely mentioned during the Christmas season. But every year, on December 28, the daily Catholic Mass is offered in remembrance of the babies and toddlers who involuntarily gave their lives to protect the Holy Family.[14] Perhaps all Christians should pause every year, on December 28, to remember these largely unsung heroes who gave their lives to protect the baby Jesus at such a young age. The trauma that all of those unsuspecting families must have experienced is undeniable.

***

In Jerusalem, during the very early days of the church in the first century, church members were expected to renounce attachment to material possessions and property. Scripture tells us that

> the multitude of them that believed were of one heart
> and of one soul: neither said any of them that ought of
> the things which he possessed was his own; but they

had all things common.

Acts 4:32. During this period,

> as many as were possessors of lands or houses sold
> them, and brought the prices of the things that were
> sold, and laid them down at the apostles' feet: and dis-
> tribution was made unto every man according as he
> had need.

Acts 4:34-35.

During this time in Jerusalem—when all the members of the
church were selling their possessions and donating all of the proceeds
to the church—Scripture tells us of a very disturbing incident. There
was a married couple, Ananias & Sapphira, who "sold a possession,
And kept back part of the price." *Acts 5:1-2.* St. Peter, whom Jesus had
personally made the leader of the apostles, *Matthew 16:18-19*, somehow
knew that the couple had deceptively held on to some of the purchase
price they received for their possession. There was apparently an understanding that the couple would be donating the *whole* purchase price
to the church.

The husband, Ananias, came into the church and brought "part of
the price" he received for some land, and "laid it at the apostles' feet."
Acts 5:1-2. Peter then said to him:

> Ananias, why hath Satan filled thine heart to lie to the
> Holy Ghost, and to keep back part of the price of the
> land? Whiles it remained, was it not thine own? and
> after it was sold, was it not in thine own power? why
> hast thou conceived this thing in thine heart? Thou
> hast not lied unto men, but unto God.

Acts 5:3-4. After Peter said this, Ananias was so traumatized, that he
"fell down and gave up the ghost." *Acts 5:5.* Some "young men arose,
wound him up, and carried him out, and buried him." *Acts 5:6.*

About three hours later, Ananias's wife, Sapphira, came into the
church, probably looking for her husband, who by then had been gone
for a while. Peter asked her how much they got for the land that they

sold. Sapphira lied and told Peter the lower amount, which Ananias had already donated. *Acts 5:8*. Peter then said to her,

> How is it that ye have agreed together to tempt the Spirit of the Lord? behold, the feet of them which have buried thy husband are at the door, and shall carry thee out.

Acts 5:9. Then, she fell down at Peter's feet, "and yielded up the ghost: and the young men came in, and found her dead, and, carrying her forth, buried her by her husband." *Acts 5:10*.

This story became widely spread. Scripture says that "great fear came upon all the church, and upon as many as heard these things." *Acts 5:11*. The telling of this incident—including its inclusion in the New Testament—was apparently done for the specific purpose of traumatizing church members everywhere.

My inner Genesis 18 Abraham asks, "Did the Holy Spirit actually kill these people like that? Over a dispute about money? And wasn't Peter a little harsh, especially in consideration of the fact that, not long before this incident, he denied knowing Jesus no less than three times?"

During the Last Supper, Jesus knew that after he got arrested, Peter was going to deny knowing him three times. Jesus even told Peter as much. *Matthew 26:34*. Jesus was later arrested and brought to the palace of Caiaphas, the high priest. Peter followed Jesus and the men who arrested him secretly from afar to the high priest's palace and mingled with his servants outside of the palace "to see the end." *Matthew 26:57-58*. Some of the servants gathered around Peter because they recognized him as one of Jesus's disciples. They asked him if he was a disciple of Jesus. Sure enough, as Jesus knew would happen, Peter denied him three times.

> But he denied before them all, saying, I know not what thou sayest. ... And again he denied with an oath, I do not know the man. ... Then began he to curse and to swear, saying, I know not the man.

Matthew 26:69-75.

Peter denied knowing Jesus under oath. Oaths were serious business for the people of the Bible. Someone making a statement under oath was asking God to curse them and punish them if they were lying. Therefore, if nothing bad happened to them, this was seen as God vouching for them, that they were telling the truth. Peter used God as a witness that he was telling the truth when he in fact was lying. The Risen Jesus is said to have specifically forgiven Peter for denying him by asking Peter, a symbolical three times, if Peter loved him. Each time, Peter answered that he indeed loved Jesus. After each of Peter's three affirmative answers, Jesus responded, "Feed my lambs. ... Feed my sheep. ... Feed my sheep." *John 21:15-17.*

In light of Peter's having sworn by God to a lie—and how Jesus forgave him for doing so—there was a noticeable lack of introspective self-awareness on Peter's part during the Ananias and Sapphira incident. Peter did not seem interested in paying forward the forgiveness that he received from Jesus for swearing by God that he did not know him. Ananias lied about a monetary sum. Peter threw Jesus under the bus at the lowest point in Jesus's life. He swore by God that he didn't know him. Which is worse?

If this story were not in the Bible, and someone were to suggest today that the Holy Spirit once sanctioned and caused the death of two people simply for donating less to their church than they had pledged to do, many would accuse that someone of blasphemy for suggesting such a thing. But, yet, there it is, right there in the Bible. Today, this story is largely glossed over because most church leaders don't know what to do with it.

Put yourself in the position of an outsider to the church when this incident occurred. You casually observe this couple walking into a church, one after the other about three hours apart. You also observe that not very long after each of them entered the church, their dead bodies were carried out of the church. What conclusion would *you* draw at that point? ...I'll just leave that right there.

It is up to each of us to decide what we make of this story, what we think it means, and whether we believe it. It explicitly says right there in the Scripture passage that this incident traumatized those in the church and everyone who heard about it. *Acts 5:11.* The telling of this story was intentionally meant to traumatize its hearers.

***

The God in whom I believe would not intentionally traumatize anyone. But people *can* be traumatized by their own impression of God. Especially vulnerable are children who can be traumatized by God, as they imagine God to be.

Religious parents and religious educators need to be very careful about what we teach children about God, and how we do it. As adults, it is easy for us to forget how differently a child perceives the world around them than we do as adults. Children can be easily frightened by a story that an adult doesn't think twice about. The imagination of a child can be easily sparked by the slightest suggestions.

Little children are taught the story of Noah's Ark. There are many children's books designed to tell them the story. I know that most people do the best they can to tell it in a way that is gentle and loving for the kids. But there's only so much spinning they can do to soften the fact that it's a story about how God felt so grieved, that he killed all but eight people in the entire world. Is it a mischaracterization to refer to the story of Noah's Ark as being about mass genocide?

God killed almost everyone in the world. It rained and rained, and all the people died in a flood. But don't worry, kids, God loves you, he just hated all those people back then. They were really bad. No need to freak out every time we get heavy rain or flooding, though.

Then, kids, there's the story of how God asked a Dad to kill his son. And he agreed to do it! God stopped him just in time, though. But, don't worry kids, God would never ask your Dad to kill you.

Then kids, there's the story about how God hardened the heart of the king of Egypt so that he persistently refused to let the Israelite slaves go free. So, in retaliation for his stubbornness, from God having hardened his heart, God killed the firstborn sons of all the Egyptians. Not just Pharaoh's firstborn son—all the Egyptians' firstborn sons. But, don't worry kids, God would never kill you as punishment for any bad thing that God makes the leader of your country do.

Many traumatizing stories and incidents in the Bible are collectively ignored by believers and the shepherds who lead them. But certain traumatic Bible stories are so central to the overarching history of salvation that, I guess, they cannot be ignored. Perhaps the stories must be told, even to young children. Noah's Ark, the sacrifice of Isaac, and the death of the firstborn in Egypt are probably among those stories. And nothing is more traumatic in the Bible than the Passion of Jesus and his death on the Cross. But Christians can't very well omit *that*. But do these stories contribute to and further cause childhood trauma?

Let's be honest. Many of us teach our children about a God who does a *lot* of killing. Included in all of the killing, is the mixed message "greatest story ever told" where we teach children that God loves them, but in order to let them into heaven, God had to make his Son suffer brutal torture and death. We tell children that Jesus died for *them*. Jesus died for *their* sins. A child may very well think, "Aww. Jesus died because of *me*? It's *my* fault?"

Many children are traumatized if their parents divorce because they think the divorce was their fault. How much more trauma may be involved if they walk around thinking that the suffering and death of Jesus was their fault.

If we do not believe that children can be traumatized by being told these stories about God killing people, then we are seriously underestimating the capacity of children to think and reflect for themselves. In the child's mind, because of these stories, God can fall into the same category as a parent who tells the child that they love them, but also engages in abusive behavior. Such a parent is never fully trusted by the child. The child learns to modify how they behave, and perhaps who they are, so as not to trigger more angry abuse from their parent.

A child can form an impression of God as someone who cannot be fully trusted to not go off the handle. A child's impression of God can go on to traumatize that child, maybe for the rest of their life.

***

The Bible identifies inherited generational trauma from its very beginnings. The trauma—consisting largely of a feeling of abandonment, rejection, and betrayal from God and others—started right there in the Garden of Eden, and spread from there.

In the chapters ahead, we'll follow the course of the generational trauma from its inception in the Garden to its apex on the Cross. We'll see how Scripture specifically shows us how negative parental traits were passed down from generation to generation. Scripture refers to this as the passing down of the sins of the fathers. The Church refers to this as original sin.

According to Scripture, the tendency to sin—i.e., engage in maladaptive behavior—is an inherited trait. Many of the authors of the Bible knew this. They had the consideration, foresight, wisdom, and discipline to take the time to leave a record of their observations about their trauma—as well as many other things—for future generations.

As we take a close look at some specific Bible stories, be sure to put on your Genesis 18 Abraham, and let your own conscience speak to you. Think for yourself about what the Bible says.

We begin—where else?—In the beginning...

The Rebuke of Adam & Eve
Charles-Joseph Natoire (1700-1777)

CHAPTER SIX

ADAM & EVE

"And the LORD *God said,*
Behold, the man is become as one of us, to know good and evil."
-- Genesis 3:22

———

THE GENESIS CREATION and Eden passages—traditionally authored by Moses—took stories inherited from the ancient Sumerians to whole new levels.[1] In order to explain the trauma and suffering in the world, these scriptural passages told a story of how the very first human beings suffered trauma at the hands of God. Even though the Garden of Eden would eventually become known as a paradise, it is interesting to note that Scripture does not include an account of even one joyful or blissful day experienced by Adam and Eve there. Not one. The words love or joy are not mentioned in the story at all.

Most Bible scholars today do not believe that Adam or Eve were actual historical figures. I agree with them. They represent our first parents, whoever they may have actually been. But, for the purposes of getting at the intent and purpose of the narrative, I discuss their story at face value.

***

It is apparent that Adam and Eve were not perfect when they were created. They must have had flaws even before their fall from grace. Otherwise, they would not have been so easily swayed by the serpent in the garden. They apparently already had some level of fear and distrust of God from the get go. They were very easily convinced to distrust and disobey God.

According to the story, they were created directly by God as adults. They were not raised by any human parents. They had no childhood traumas. Their only "parent" was God. So, if they had any trauma or dysfunctionality which they passed on to their offspring, that trauma could only have come from God. They were traumatized by their own distorted view of God, which they seemed to possess from the beginning. Whatever may have transpired, it seems clear that the relationship that Adam and Eve had with God was not good. And it was never good.

The relationship between Adam & Eve and God was poisoned very early on in the story. When asked by the serpent about what God said to her about the fruit of the tree in the middle of the garden, Eve told the serpent that God said, "Ye shall not eat of it, neither shall you touch it, lest ye die." *Genesis 3:3*. Eve actually misquotes God here. God never said they weren't allowed to *touch* the fruit. God merely said they weren't allowed to *eat* the fruit, "for in the day that thou eatest thereof thou shalt surely die." *Genesis 2:17*. This misquote reveals an early tendency on Eve's part to think of God as being more harsh and more restrictive than he actually was with them. In her mind, Eve was already afraid of God to some extent. So, playing on her already existing distorted image of God, the serpent sought to further damage her view of God and her relationship with him.

The serpent fostered a deeper distrust of God in Eve, which added to her fear of him. The serpent flat out calls God a liar by telling her, "Ye shall not surely die." *Genesis 3:4*. The serpent then goes on to convey to Eve that God has spurious motives and that God did not have Eve's best interests at heart.

The serpent told Eve, "For God doth know that in the day ye eat thereof, then your eyes shall be opened, and ye shall be as gods, knowing good and evil." *Genesis 3:5*. Most people believe this to have been a lie from the serpent. ...But was it? *Genesis 3:22*.

As the story goes, Adam and Eve both ate of the forbidden fruit of the tree. *Genesis 3:6*. As a result, "they knew that they were naked." *Genesis 3:7*. Later, when they heard the sound of God approaching them in the garden, "Adam and his wife hid themselves from the presence of the LORD God amongst the trees of the garden." *Genesis 3:8*. In other words, they experienced shame. This can be viewed as the first case of what is referred to today as toxic shame.[2] Adam and Eve were ashamed of who they were, not of any particular thing that they had done. Yes, they ate the forbidden fruit in disobedience to God. But, as a result of that, their eyes were opened so that they could see themselves as they really were, i.e., "naked." They didn't like what they saw. They were ashamed of what they saw. They loathed themselves.

At this point, this became a dysfunctional relationship between our first parents and their Creator. It got to the point where Adam and Eve viewed God with suspicion, distrust, and fear. God's very presence filled them with a sense of shame—toxic shame. They experienced trauma, for which they blamed God.

***

In the New Testament, St. Paul definitely had an axe to grind against Eve as opposed to Adam. He clearly believed both of them to be historical figures. Paul spoke of Adam as a foreshadow or prefiguration of Christ. *Romans 5:12-14.* He likened and juxtaposed Adam with Christ when he wrote: "For as in Adam, all die, even so in Christ shall all be made alive." *1 Corinthians 15:22.* He referred to Christ as "the last Adam." *1 Corinthians 15:45.* In so closely linking Adam to Jesus, Adam had a place of honor in Paul's telling of the history of salvation. *2 Corinthians 11:3.* He exonerates Adam by saying that "Adam was not deceived, but the woman being deceived was in the transgression." *1 Timothy 2:14.* It was not Adam who was duped by the serpent—it was his wife.

***

My earliest memory is of meeting Adam. I wasn't quite sure how we met. It was just like all of a sudden, I was there out of nowhere. I didn't appreciate it then, but we lived in a beautiful garden. We were kicked out of there and I never lived in a place as beautiful as that again. I remember not being sure why I was there. I mean, it was just the two of them I knew in the garden. There was Adam, and there was God. From the beginning, I wasn't really sure about my relationship with either of them.

I remember figuring out very early on that Adam seemed to believe that he was in charge of me, and God seemed to be in charge of Adam. I wasn't sure that I wanted either one of them in charge of me. I wasn't sure if I wanted anything to do with either of them. I remember wondering what that whole situation in the garden was all about. I was afraid.

I had so many questions. Who am I? Where did I come from? What am I doing here? Can you imagine walking around every day with no idea who you are or what your life is all about? That was me. Completely clueless. There I was, with no idea why.

One day, Adam told me that we were free to eat the fruit from any tree in the garden, except the most beautiful one in the middle of the garden. He told me that God gave him that instruction before we met.[3] That's when I began to realize that God was in charge and that there was a pecking order—God, then Adam, then me.[4] I asked Adam why I wasn't allowed to eat from that beautiful tree. He told me not to eat from it and to not even touch it![5] He told me that God said if we ate from the tree, we would die. I didn't even know what that meant. The whole concept of dying was a big mystery to me.

Was the tree poisonous? Why can't we eat its fruit? I didn't get it.

Adam told me that God planted the whole garden himself. I remember thinking—after Adam told me we weren't allowed to eat the fruit from the tree—that if God didn't want us eating from that tree, then why did he plant it in the garden in the first place? Good question. Am I right? It's all so confusing.

I remember thinking that Adam was rather stern with me. I didn't say anything at the time, and I kept my thoughts to myself, but I remember I was a bit angry with Adam, and with God too.

Who put Adam in charge?

God?

Well, who put God in charge?

I was getting fed up with both of them.

I used to go off on my own for long stretches of time so that I could have time for myself. You know what I mean? Alone time. No Adam. No God.

So, one day while I was sitting alone, I met this serpent. The serpent befriended me. We would have these long conversations. He talked <u>with</u> me, not <u>at</u> me. He never ordered me around. He never told me what to do. He just spent time with me. I liked him.

You know what I liked best about the serpent? He made me <u>think</u>. He asked me questions that made me ponder things and made me realize that I could think for myself. ...Me![6] He made me realize that I have a mind! He would ask <u>me</u> what <u>I</u> think!

I told him how I felt about Adam ordering me around and how God told us not to eat the fruit from that beautiful tree in the middle of the garden. He sympathized with me. I felt like he was the only one who really understood me.

I miss our talks.

So, after I told the serpent about God commanding us not to eat the fruit from the tree, the serpent laughed, rolled his eyes and said, "Wow! He really said that? He said you're not allowed to eat from any of the trees in the garden?" I told him, no, that we were just not allowed to eat from the tree in the middle of the garden, or even touch it, or we would die that day.[7] The serpent laughed and scoffed at that. He told me that we would surely <u>not</u> die.[8]

And then he told me something really interesting.

The serpent said that God wasn't being honest with us. He said that the <u>real</u> reason God didn't want us to eat from the tree in the middle of the garden is because, if we did, our eyes would be opened and that we would be just like gods, knowing good from evil.[9]

Hmm. ...That really made me think.

The serpent said the fruit of the tree would make me wise. I liked that. I liked the idea of being wise and knowledgeable. It was appealing to me.

...I ate the fruit.

I must say, it made me feel great! I never felt so empowered before. I went home and convinced Adam to eat the fruit.[10] I could do that because, after eating the fruit, I immediately became much smarter and wiser than him. He was easily swayed by me to take the fruit.

God was angry that we ate the fruit. His anger frightened me. I'd never seen God that angry before. He yelled at us. He put a curse on the serpent. He put a curse on me, saying that I would experience great pain every time I gave birth. I didn't even know what giving birth was at the time!

There I was cowering, being yelled at and cursed, completely naked, scared out of my mind. And for what? What did I do wrong? I wanted to be smarter and wiser![11] Is that so wrong?

And you know, everybody says that the serpent is an evil liar, and that no one should ever believe him. He told me that if we ate the fruit, that our eyes would be open and that we would be just like gods, knowing good from evil.[12] Was that a lie? Well, after God yelled at us and cursed us, I overheard him speaking with someone. I'm not sure who he was talking to, but God himself said that because we ate the fruit, we had become just like him knowing good from evil![13] *What?! That's what the serpent said would happen!*[14] *Who's the liar then? ...I was so confused.*

The funny thing is that everyone thinks that I lived in a paradise. But honestly, looking back, my entire time there with God in that garden was filled with fear, anger, and anxiety almost every day. Ultimately, my time there, and my expulsion from the garden, left me with feelings of abandonment and betrayal from God.

***

The creation and Eden passages are the Scripture's very first account of the Abrahamic/Mosaic God's relationship with his people. What it tells is a story of how our first parents felt unloved, abandoned, and betrayed by God. Modern psychology would refer to this story as being about abandonment anxiety.[15] Just as there are many children who fear being abandoned by their parents,[16] in the Bible there is a long string of people, spanning multiple generations, who felt abandoned and betrayed by God. This includes Jesus. According to the Gospels of Matthew and Mark, Jesus's last words before dying on the Cross were, "My God, my God, why hast thou forsaken me?" *Matthew 27:46; Mark 15:34.*

Abandonment and betrayal by God is a recurring theme throughout Scripture. This should not be overlooked, ignored, or otherwise glossed over. From beginning to end, the Bible depicts how even the most prominent biblical figures went through periods of feeling abandoned and betrayed by God. This was their fear. This was their trauma.

The fallout from feeling traumatized, by the sense of abandonment and betrayal from God, would then be passed down from Adam and Eve to their descendants through the process of inherited generational trauma.

Adam and Eve went on to have children, including Cain and Abel. The epic saga continues...

CHAPTER SEVEN

CAIN & ABEL

"Am I my brother's keeper?"
-- Genesis 4:9

———

ADAM AND EVE went on to give birth to their first two sons. Cain, and then later Abel. Cain grew up to be a farmer, while Abel grew up to be a shepherd. *Genesis 4:1-2.*

At some point, both Cain and Abel brought gifts to God. Cain brought God a gift "of the fruit of the ground," but Abel brought God a gift "of the firstlings of his flock and of the fat thereof." *Genesis 4:3-4.* Apparently, Abel gave God a gift from the best of his stock, while Cain just picked a mediocre offering of the fruit of the ground. But, whatever the reason, God

> had respect unto Abel and to his offering: But unto
> Cain and to his offering he had not respect. And Cain
> was very wroth, and his countenance fell.

Genesis 4:4-5. Was Cain right to be angry? Well, perhaps he already perceived some favoritism on the part of his parents toward Abel, so that when God apparently showed some favoritism toward Abel, it infuriated Cain. Cain killed Abel for this reason. *Genesis 4:8.* Whatever the specific circumstances, it is clear that humanity's first murder, according to the story, was the result of a dysfunctional family dynamic brought upon by generational trauma. This would go on to be the first in a long line of generations in Scripture to be so affected.

I think it's safe to say that anyone who commits cold blooded murder suffers from some form of mental illness. The first murder in the biblical saga was committed by someone just one generation shy of the very first humans. It did not take long at all for the original trauma to have such a tragic effect.

***

As far back as I can remember, my mother would periodically tell me these stories about her experiences in the garden where my parents used to live. My dad didn't talk about those days so much. But my mother obviously never got over what happened to her there. She would go on and on about her days there.

Mom was really angry with God. And she was angry at my father too for taking God's side much of the time and letting God treat us so badly. Dad just stood by and let God yell at them and curse them and throw them out of the garden and all that. Mom says he was afraid to stand up to God. Yeah, Mom took shots at Dad's manhood a lot for that.

Mom also sometimes went on and on about this guy she called the Serpent. She says they had great conversations. She says that he really understood her and made her feel smart, more confident, and less afraid. She says that God and Dad always made her feel like dirt, and that she was always kind of scared of the both of them. The way she constantly talked about that Serpent guy made me feel like Mom had a thing for him. In fact, I've heard rumors that the Serpent is actually my real Dad.[1] ...Seriously, people say that.

God once told me that my dad, Adam, is my real biological father. But I remember that my mom used to say that God lies. So, who knows?

I think Dad always suspected that maybe he wasn't my real father. Maybe that's why my brother Abel was always his favorite. I remember growing up feeling very angry with Abel because I felt Dad's favoritism towards him constantly. It was palpable. Maybe that's why I spent so much of my time with Mom. She seemed to love me well enough.

I know that there are people who believe that the Serpent is my real father. And, since everyone seems to think of the Serpent as this bad dude, even evil incarnate, that makes me a bad seed in their eyes. A really bad seed. It's hard to shake that bad seed label, though, given the fact that I killed my own brother.

...I killed my own brother.

You know, when I hear myself say it out loud like that, it sounds really, really bad.

I'm not precisely sure what made me do it. I'm not even sure if I'm sorry I did it. If given the chance to go back in time and relive that day over again, would I refrain from killing him? Maybe. I remember being blinded by anger and rage toward Abel.

God triggered my anger and rage toward Abel.

...Yes, I blame God.

God cursed me for killing Abel. He was cursing all of us left and right back then. He said that I would be a fugitive and a vagabond for the rest of my life.[2] At first, I protested that this punishment was more than I could bear. But—then again—I did kill my brother.

Interestingly enough, even though I killed someone, God did say he would protect me from being killed.[3] I thought that was pretty cool. I'll give him that much.

Abel loved God because he wasn't as close to Mom as I was, being Dad's favorite and all. He was closer to Dad than he was with Mom. He didn't speak with Mom much.

I, on the other hand, spent a lot of time with Mom, listening to her stories about God and Dad and the Serpent and the garden. Mom's negative talk about God made me think less of him, and less of Dad as well, to be honest.

I remember that Abel and I both brought God these gifts. I forget the occasion. Actually, I didn't feel like bringing God a gift at all. But Abel— Abel loved God. Me, I had my misgivings about him.

Whatever impressions I had of God came from Mom.

Abel spent a lot of time preparing his gift for God. I, on the other hand, dragged my feet preparing his gift and just put something together at the last second. I thought for a while about not giving God a gift at all. But, you know, given what Mom told me about his temper and all, I didn't want to offend. So, we both gave our gifts to God.

I noticed, when God received both of our gifts, that he really liked Abel's gift, but not mine. He made a face when he looked at my gift. I asked him if there was anything wrong with my gift. He gave me no answer to that. Sensing that I was getting mad, he just told me not to be angry and that I should try to give him a better gift next time. Seriously, that made me even more angry.

I think what triggered my anger was that God showed blatant favor- itism toward Abel. Favoritism toward Abel was a serious issue for me since childhood. I think I was about six years old when Abel was born. I'm not sure. He became the instant favorite. I think it's possible that Dad thought of me as the Serpent's son, making Abel therefore his real firstborn son. I could be wrong about all of that. But I don't think that I am.

Killing my brother makes me the world's first murderer.

Yay!

…I know, it's a dubious distinction at best.

***

Cain and Abel were an example of sibling rivalry taken to its extreme. The most common causes of sibling rivalry are jealousy and competition. This is usually caused by the perception of one sibling that the other is receiving more love and attention from a parent.[4] In the biblical story, God clearly showed favoritism toward Abel. *Genesis 4:4-5.* The Abrahamic/Mosaic God gave Cain feelings of abandonment and betrayal. Cain perceived God as being unsupportive at best. It should be noted that Scripture explicitly states that the first act of violence, from one human to another, happened because the perpetrator felt ill-treated by God.

Research shows that jealousy is among the top reasons that people commit murder. People get jealous of what others have, or how life seems to be treating them with an unfair advantage. (Being treated with favoritism by God?) Scripture accurately described the reason why many murders occur, even today. And get this—research shows that 91% of men and 84% of women have had thoughts of killing someone, including planning their hypothetical homicides in considerable detail.[5] This is a frightening statistic. Another frightening statistic is that some one-third of all murders in the United States goes unsolved.[6] In 2020, during the pandemic, the percentage of unsolved murders rose to half.[7]

***

Some eight generations after them, Adam and Eve became ancestors of the protagonist of the story of the Great Flood—Noah.[8]

The inherited generational trauma continued forward.

CHAPTER EIGHT

NOAH AND HIS SONS

"Heaven and earth shall pass away, but my words shall not pass away. But of that day and hour knoweth no man, no, not the angels of heaven, but my Father only. But as the days of [Noah] were, so shall also the coming of the Son of man be. For as in the days that were before the flood they were eating and drinking, marrying and giving in marriage, until the day that [Noah] entered into the ark, And knew not until the flood came, and took them all away; so shall also the coming of the Son of man be. Then shall two be in the field; the one shall be taken, and the other left. Two women shall be grinding at the mill; the one shall be taken, and the other left. Watch therefore: for ye know not what hour your Lord doth come."

-- Matthew 24:35-42

THE STORY OF Noah begins when the Abrahamic/Mosaic God decides to destroy all of humanity because "GOD saw that the wickedness of man was great in the earth, and that every imagination of the thoughts of his heart was only evil continually." *Genesis 6:5*. God was sorry that he created humans at all. *Genesis 6:6*.

The Scripture says that "it repented the LORD that he had made man on the earth, and it grieved him at his heart." *Genesis 6:6*. The Hebrew word for grieved in this passage is נחם, pronounced *naw-kham'*.[1] This word refers to a sense of very deep grief and compassion. The Scripture here portrays God as being deeply hurt the way someone can feel wounded and betrayed by someone that they love. So, the feeling of betrayal between humans and God was mutual. The Abrahamic/Mosaic God is a God who lashes out when he feels hurt and betrayed.

The proverbial shoe is on the other foot here, in that it is now God who is hurt by feelings of betrayal. God's people have rejected him. They are living lives of complete wickedness, ignoring his very existence. *Genesis 6:5*. God's feelings are hurt. *Genesis 6:6*. The Abrahamic/Mosaic God is a jealous God. *Exodus 34:14*. God is experiencing jealousy.

My Genesis 18 Abraham makes me think that an omniscient and omnipotent God would be above all of this stuff. Would a true God be jealous and lash out, in an emotional overreaction, after experiencing rejection from his people? God's decision to flood the earth is similar to how some people lash out after experiencing interpersonal rejection, low perceived relational value, and jealousy.[2] Would a perfect, eternal God have this type of psychological issue? Of course not. But this depiction of God is an *impression* of God. This is the Abrahamic/Mosaic God. This depiction of God reflects on the psychology of the original tellers of this story. They were okay worshipping a God who thought and behaved this way.

It is worth noting that, at this point, very early on in Scripture—at just the sixth chapter of Genesis—the Bible depicts a relationship between God and his people that is permeated with mutual distrust and antipathy. The people rejected God and, by his flood, God rejected his people. The flood, though, solved nothing. The descendants of Noah would go on to be just as sinful and wicked as the people killed in the flood. Murders and other crimes would continue. One would think that God would know that this would be the case.

Killing people solves nothing. But this did not stop God from going on to destroy Sodom and Gomorrah, kill all of the firstborn in Egypt, and encourage war after war against people who didn't believe in him.[3] God's *modus operandi* seems to have been to kill, kill, kill, until people got the message—which they never really did.

The flood is depicted in Scripture as the lashing out of a God that was "grieved" by his people. *Genesis 6:6*. This impression of God apparently sat well enough with the first readers of the story. I would think, however, using my Genesis 18 Abraham, that the true God would be above this kind of thing.

***

There are many passages in the Bible that, over time, have caused me to pause and ponder. Genesis 6:6 is one of them. This portrait of an omniscient God regretting that he had done something—acknowledging it as a mistake—can be confusing to those of us who believe that God is perfect and would never do something he would later feel repentant about. But then this raises a question. Is the Abrahamic/Mosaic God of the Bible truly omniscient?

King David, while contemplating the knowledge of God, is said to have written: "Such knowledge is too wonderful for me; it is high; I cannot attain unto it." *Psalm 139:6*. But just because God's knowledge is beyond our understanding doesn't necessarily mean that God is omniscient. It can simply just mean that God knows everything that we know and more.

Scripture also says: "Great is our Lord, and of great power: his understanding is infinite." *Psalm 147:5*. However, the word infinite here is the Hebrew word מִסְפָּר, pronounced *mis-pawr'*, which refers to mathematical enumeration.[4] In other places in Scripture, this word has been translated as "few *in number*," *Genesis 34:30*, "without *number*," *Genesis 41:49*, "according to *the number*," *Exodus 16:16*, and the like. What the Psalmist is saying here is that God's understanding is without measure and incalculable for us. But, one can argue that just because God's understanding is incalculable and without measure doesn't necessarily mean that he's omniscient. It just means that we are incapable of measuring, quantifying, or otherwise grasping the full extent of his knowledge and wisdom.

The people in the days of the Old Testament probably did not have the same understanding of the word infinite as we have today. Their closest understanding to infinity might have been the idea of a very long time. The idea of infinity as referring to the non-existence of time probably did not occur to them.

It is the same with omniscience. The concept of infinite knowledge, as we would understand it, probably didn't occur to the people in the days of the Bible either. As immeasurable as the Scripture describes the knowledge of God, at times the Old Testament clearly places limits on God's knowledge as well. God seemed surprised when Adam and Eve disobeyed him and ate from the forbidden fruit. *Genesis 3:9-13*. King David wrote: "The LORD looked down from heaven upon the children of men, **to see if** there were any that did understand, and seek God." *Psalm 14:2* (emphasis added). An omniscient God would not need "to see" if anything was the case. An omniscient God would simply know.

The omniscience of God is a matter that has been expounded upon by great minds for thousands of years—theologians, philosophers, saints...etc. The people in the days of the Bible did not have the benefit of inheriting the wisdom of these great minds regarding ideas of God.

The operative point is not whether God is actually omniscient. The operative point is that the writers of the Bible did not think of God as omniscient because they couldn't grasp that concept. So, the idea of God getting to the point of regretting that he created human beings seemed plausible to them. *Genesis 6:6.*

***

The Great Flood happens, it rains for forty days, the earth remains flooded for one hundred and fifty days, and then the waters recede. *Genesis 7:1-8:19.* Sometime after the flood, Noah became a farmer who planted a vineyard. *Genesis 9:20.* Apparently Noah became addicted to the wine he made from his grapes and developed what we might call today a drinking problem or alcoholism. One day Noah became drunk on wine and passed out. *Genesis 9:21.* Noah's son, Ham, found his father drunk, naked, and passed out in his tent. But, instead of showing some discretion by protecting his father's honor and privacy, Ham went and "told his two brethren without." *Genesis 9:22.* At some point, Noah realized what Ham had done to him, and placed a curse on Ham and his descendants. *Genesis 9:24-25.* This is an example of a generational curse. Noah placed a curse on his own son and his descendants. This included Noah's own grandchildren and great-grandchildren.

Although the Bible does not provide us with any other accounts of Noah getting drunk like this, it is probably not too much of a stretch to suggest that this was not the first time he was so inebriated. It may be the case that Noah had a drinking problem or full-blown alcoholism. If he had a drinking problem while his sons were still children, there can be little doubt that his problem affected his family in the same way that any alcoholic would cause problems within their family. That being said, what Ham did to his father was indeed disrespectful. Maybe Ham did what he did because this was a regular occurrence with Noah. Maybe he said to his brothers, "Guys, he's plastered again!" We clearly have a dysfunctional family situation here.[5]

However, despite whatever flaws Noah may have had, it didn't stop him from finding favor with God. *Genesis 6:8*. In fact, the Bible says that the Abrahamic/Mosaic God let every other human perish in the Great Flood except for Noah and his family. *Genesis 7:7*. It is the case, with most of the flawed fathers mentioned in this book, that God showed mercy toward them and used them in mighty ways. Most of them have places of honor in the saga of the Scriptures. The most notable case of this is King David who is known in the Bible as a man after God's own heart, *Acts 13:22*, even though he committed adultery and then committed murder in an attempt to cover up the adultery, *2 Samuel 12:1-15*. Why so much mercy for these individuals? Despite his inclination to express his anger, God is also portrayed as having compassion. Maybe God's compassion stems precisely from the fact that, through no fault of their own, each of these individuals in these stories inherited trauma from their ancestors before them. And maybe, as the Bible authors subtly imply, God realized that this was at least partly his fault.

***

If we look closely at these stories so far, starting from the Garden of Eden up to Noah, there is in them an undeniable passive-aggressive blaming of God for all of the world's troubles. It's subtle, but it's there. It's almost as if the authors of the Bible—traditionally Moses in the case of the Torah—ostensibly set out to write favorably about the God they worshipped and served, but maybe they had an underlying enmity towards God that came out in their writings in various ways, perhaps subconsciously.

A close reading of the story of the expulsion of Adam and Eve from the Garden of Eden portrays God as being overly harsh with them, and shows that the serpent actually told Eve the truth. Specifically, the serpent told the truth on two counts.

First, Eve told the serpent that God said that she and Adam should not eat the fruit, or else they would die *that day*. God specifically said that "in the day that thou eatest thereof thou shalt surely die." *Genesis 2:17*. But Eve, then Adam, ate of the fruit, and they did *not* die that day. *Genesis 3:6*. So, according to the way the story reads, the serpent actually told the truth when he told Eve, "Ye shall not surely die." *Genesis 3:4.*

According to a literal reading of Scripture, Adam lived on to the age of 930. *Genesis 5:5.* Scripture does not say when Eve died. But neither one of them is said to have died after eating the fruit. In fact, the Scripture alludes to the fact that they both went on to live long and potentially fruitful lives.

The argument can be made that eating the fruit brought death into the world in the first place—that Adam and Eve were both created as immortal beings and they brought eventual death upon themselves by eating the fruit. *Romans 5:12.* But the Old Testament does not spell this out. The fact remains that, according to the account in Genesis, Adam & Eve did not die "in the day" that they ate the fruit. *Genesis 2:17.*

Second, regarding eating the fruit, the serpent told Eve, "For God doth know that in the day ye eat thereof, then your eyes shall be opened, and ye shall be as gods, knowing good and evil." *Genesis 3:5.* This was also the truth. After Adam and Eve ate the fruit, God is quoted as saying, "Behold, the man is become like one of us, to know good and evil." *Genesis 3:22.*[6] Here, we have God portrayed as *admitting* that what the serpent told Eve was true.

Then, Scripture subtly blames God for triggering the murder of Abel by Cain. *Genesis 4:5.* According to Scripture, the murder of Abel ushered violence and murder into the world. God showed blatant favoritism towards Abel. And then, the omniscient God seemed surprised at what he had driven Cain to do. *Genesis 4:9.*[7] When violence in the world got out of hand, *Genesis 6:11*, God decides to kill everything with a flood and start fresh—a plan that did not work at all. Violence, murders, wars…etc., all went on after the flood.

At the very least, these stories do not portray God in a very flattering way.

***

Noah's sons had children, and their children had children. Eventually, some twelve generations after him, Noah becomes an ancestor of the Bible's most prolific patriarch—Abraham.[8]

CHAPTER NINE

ABRAHAM AND ISAAC

"The father of the righteous shall greatly rejoice:
and he that begetteth a wise child shall have joy of him."
-- Proverbs 23:24

―――――

S CRIPTURE TELLS US almost nothing about Abraham's parents
or his life prior to his heading for the land of Canaan. *Genesis 12:1-
5.* But there are incidents from Jewish midrashic sources that give us
an interesting glimpse into the inherited generational trauma that Abraham may have suffered prior to his appearance in the biblical stories.

Abraham's father was a man named Terah. *Genesis 11:27.* Abraham
had two brothers named Nahor and Haran. Haran was the father of
Lot. *Genesis 11:31.* Lot was therefore Abraham's nephew.

Abraham's father was a chief general in the armed forces of Babylon—appointed so by Nimrod, king of Babylon.[1] He was also an idol
worshipper. *Joshua 24:2.* Not only was he an idol worshipper, he operated a business selling idols.[2]

When Abraham was born, Nimrod's stargazers warned the king
that Abraham would one day be a threat to Nimrod's throne.[3] Nimrod
ordered Terah to send him the baby because Abraham was to be put
to death.[4] Terah, however, thwarted the king's plan to put Abraham to
death. The infant Abraham, along with his mother and nurse, went
into hiding in a cave for ten years.[5]

It is said that at the age of three, Abraham was already expressing
his disdain for beliefs in idols and polytheism. Abraham expressed his
belief that there was one great God who created everything.[6] This
monotheistic God, of whom Abraham spoke, would eventually become known as the God of Abraham.

When Abraham was an adult, about the age of 50,[7] there was one incident where Terah needed to take a trip and left Abraham in charge of his shop where he sold idols.[8] Abraham, however, did not believe in these idols—in disagreement with his father—and began discouraging potential customers from buying any, thereby sabotaging his own father's business. Abraham also destroyed the idols in his father's store in iconoclastic fashion.[9]

Upon returning, and finding his idols destroyed by his son, Terah was furious. Terah reported what his son had done to King Nimrod, who sentenced Abraham to death by burning. Abraham somehow managed to escape the flames and survive. However, Abraham's brother, Haran, was thrown into the furnace and died for expressing support for his brother, Abraham.[10]

The fact that Abraham's father reported what Abraham had done to the king—thereby exposing him to the capital punishment of being burned to death—speaks volumes about their relationship. Abraham lived the rest of his life knowing that his father unsuccessfully tried to have him killed. This motif of a father almost killing his son would famously revisit Abraham down the road.

Abraham was almost burned to death because his father reported his actions to the authorities. As a result, Abraham's brother was gruesomely burned to death, instead of him, because of something that *he* did. This is the trauma that Abraham brought with him to the promised land. His trauma would, of course, go on to affect his outlook on life, and his impressions of God. His were the impressions that were handed down to Moses. Their combined impressions would go on to form the Abrahamic/Mosaic God, which became the widely accepted impression of God adopted by more than half of the world.

***

When Abraham reached a certain age, he complained to God about being childless. *Genesis 15:2*. God promised Abraham that he would have an heir. *Genesis 15:4*. Abraham fathered a child with a woman named Hagar. He named his son Ishmael. *Genesis 16:15*. Abraham finally had an heir—or so he thought. But God told Abraham that Ishmael was not the heir he promised him. God specifically tells Abraham that Isaac was to be his rightful heir, a son to be born to Sarah, his wife. *Genesis 17:18-21.*[11]

Abraham's relationship with his son, Isaac, is an interesting one. At one point—after making Abraham wait so long for an heir—God decides to test Abraham by asking him to kill Isaac as a burnt offering. *Genesis 22:2.* Abraham was to burn Isaac to death, just as his father wanted to burn *him* to death.

On the way to the site of the burnt offering, not yet knowing that he was supposed to be the human sacrifice, Isaac notices that they don't seem to have an animal to kill and offer up to God. Isaac asks his father, "Behold the fire and the wood: but where is the lamb for a burnt offering?" *Genesis 22:7.* Abraham does not explain to Isaac what he intends to do, but simply says cryptically, "My son, God will provide himself a lamb for a burnt offering." *Genesis 22:8.*[12] Just before Abraham was about to kill Isaac with a knife, "the angel of the LORD" calls down to Abraham from heaven and stops him from doing it. *Genesis 22:10-12.* Abraham has passed God's test of faith, loyalty, and obedience.

The fact that Abraham just blindly obeyed God when God asked him to kill his son is interesting in light of that previous conversation that Abraham had with God in Genesis 18. When God told Abraham that he intended to destroy Sodom and Gomorrah, the Genesis 18 Abraham interceded on their behalf. *Genesis 18:16-32.* Abraham challenged God to be fair and merciful rather than to indiscriminately "destroy the righteous with the wicked." *Genesis 18:23.* This prior interaction with God makes his blind obedience to God's command to kill Isaac curious. He could have protested that Isaac was innocent and did not deserve to be killed. But he did not.

When God asked Abraham to offer up Isaac as a human sacrifice, this was Abraham's own impression of what God asked him to do.

***

The killing of one's own son or daughter is called filicide. There is research which shows that there are five main motivations or reasons for filicide. The motivations or reasons for killing a child are: (1) to alleviate their real or imagined suffering; (2) due to some irrational motive; (3) because that child is perceived as a hindrance; (4) out of neglect or abuse; and (5) in order to get back at a spouse or partner.[13] Of these five reasons, Abraham may very well have been motivated by at least two of them.

Abraham may have viewed Isaac as a hindrance. In order to please his wife, Sarah, Abraham sent his firstborn son Ishmael away, along with his mother. Scripture tells us that "the thing was very grievous in Abraham's sight because of his son." *Genesis 21:11*. In the patriarchal society in which Abraham lived, a man's firstborn son meant everything to him, regardless of who the mother was. There is little doubt that Abraham had deep resentment toward Isaac, and toward Sarah for what he did to Ishmael just to accommodate her.

Abraham may have also wanted to kill Isaac to get back at Sarah. Perhaps Abraham thought he misread what he perceived that God had told him about Ishmael. Perhaps Abraham decided that he had made a huge mistake by sending Ishmael—his firstborn son—away like that. Perhaps Abraham decided that he had made a mistake by letting Sarah call the shots like that. After all, he was the man of the family in a society wherein women had no rights to speak of. Why did he let his wife push him around? Abraham's resentment toward Sarah must have been building for a while. Maybe he came to the conclusion that, because he tried to be an accommodating husband, Sarah took advantage of him.

***

Just as Abraham was about to kill Isaac, did Abraham have a moment when he asked himself, "What am I doing?!!" Did Abraham's *impression* of God at the time then tell Abraham to stop, and that it was all just a big test which Abraham had passed? And that he did not have to kill Isaac? *Genesis 22:11-12*.

Maybe Abraham sent Ishmael away, then regretted it. Then he became angry about the situation. Then he wanted to kill Isaac because of his grief over Ishmael, and his resentment towards Sarah. Then he changed his mind at the last second. Abraham attributed all of these decisions to God, rather than take responsibility for them. He thereby made God seem capricious and indecisive when, in fact, Abraham was the indecisive one.

This seems more reasonable than an omniscient, omnipotent, and omnipresent God thinking, "I'm going to test this man's loyalty by asking him to kill his beloved son for me. Let me see if he's willing to do it. No worries, though. I'm going to stop him from killing Isaac at the last second."

There is much debate about how Isaac must have felt about what his father almost did. Was Isaac angry and resentful toward Abraham for almost killing him like that? Did Isaac hear the voice of God, or did he just take Abraham at his word when Abraham said God spoke to him? Did Isaac willingly lay down to become the sacrificial burnt offering, or was he forced to do so in a physical struggle? The biblical narrative does not answer these questions. We can never know if the relationship between Abraham and Isaac ever became toxic because of this. However, it is notable that there are no recorded conversations between Abraham and Isaac in the Bible after this incident.

***

Did Isaac inherit any family trauma from Abraham? Well, Scripture tells us that Abraham told a serious lie about his wife Sarah, twice, on two separate occasions. Then Isaac told the same lie about his wife Rebekah. It is an interesting "like father like son" tale. It can be inferred here that Isaac either learned to lie in this type of situation from observing his father do it, or that he genetically inherited a propensity for lying from his father. Regardless, there are stories about Abraham, his son Isaac, and then later his grandson Jacob, which involve lies told by all three of them.

In one story, Abraham and Sarah had occasion to go down to Egypt because there was a famine in Canaan, where they lived. *Genesis 12:10-13.* When they get to Egypt, Abraham tells Sarah, his wife, to tell everyone that she was his sister. He did this because Sarah was a beautiful woman, and Abraham was afraid that some men in Egypt would be attracted to her, and kill him so that they could take Sarah as a wife. It came to pass that the ruler of Egypt, the Pharaoh, after being told that Sarah was Abraham's sister, tried to woo Sarah and almost took her as his wife. *Genesis 12:14-19.* God punishes the ruler and his house "with great plagues" because of what he was trying to do with Sarah. *Genesis 12:17.* The ruler chastised Abraham for not telling him that Sarah was his wife, and sent Abraham and Sarah on their way.

On a separate occasion, Abraham tells the same lie again to someone else! While visiting the town of Gerar, a city near the

Mediterranean, he told people that Sarah was his sister to protect himself from being killed by men who may have wanted to take her as a wife. *Genesis 20:11*. But this time, he said he wasn't really lying because he claimed that Sarah was, indeed, his half-sister, a daughter of his father but not his mother. *Genesis 20:12*. There is no confirmation of Abraham's claim elsewhere in the Bible.

The fact that Abraham did this twice shows that he had a propensity to lie, that he had cowardly traits, and that he was willing to lie to protect himself, even if it meant subjecting himself and Sarah to the dishonor of her being taken from him to be another man's wife.

Continuing this familial trait, Isaac would go on to do the same. While visiting the town of Gerar, because of a famine, Isaac claimed that Rebekah, his wife, was his sister. *Genesis 26:6-7*. However, a ruler in Gerar happened to see that "Isaac was sporting with Rebekah his wife." *Genesis 26:8*. That ruler said to Isaac,

> Behold, of a surety she is thy wife: and how saidst thou, She is my sister? ... What is this thou hast done unto us? one of the people might lightly have lien with thy wife, and thou shouldest have brought guiltiness upon us.

Genesis 26:9-10. In this scenario, the ruler of Gerar proved to have more honor and integrity than Isaac or Abraham regarding marriage and family.

The clear intention of the biblical authors/compilers, or Moses, was to show that a pattern of lying had developed in Abraham's family. They wanted to show that Abraham had a propensity to lie, and that the propensity was beginning to span generations. Why else would the Scriptures tell these unflattering stories about these patriarchs?

It is odd that these three stories of lying are so similar to each other. It is possible that the incident happened only once to either Abraham or Isaac, and that the same story was just retold under different traditions. However, these stories are being taken at face value for the purposes of this book. As such, they show a strong propensity to lie on the parts of both Abraham and Isaac.

Research shows that compulsive lying, also known as pathological lying, can be a coping mechanism for low self-esteem or past trauma.[14]

Compulsive lying is often learned by children as a way of navigating their way in a dysfunctional family that rewards lying and punishes telling one's truth.[15]

Dysfunctional families, in which abuse is going on, whether sexual or otherwise, often have enablers in the family who feel the need to cover-up the abuse and keep it a family secret. There is usually a tacit understanding in the family that the abuse is not subject to discussion. Family members are rewarded for both believing the lies which cover up the abuse, and perpetuating those same lies. The underlying threat is very clear—family whistleblowers are subject to being shunned and ostracized from the family. In such a scenario, children learn to lie for self-preservation reasons.[16]

Studies show that those who have suffered significant childhood trauma are more likely to become pathological liars.[17]

Research shows that there are five dysfunctional family traits that can cause children to become pathological liars.[18]

First, there are families wherein children are punished for telling the truth. In such a family, if a child sees something that could make the adults uncomfortable to talk about—such as abusive or dysfunctional behavior by one or both of the parents or a sibling—that child would be strongly discouraged from speaking of it. If they do speak of it, they may be punished, rejected, or ignored for it. There is an unwritten family penalty for speaking of certain things in open conversation. Children learn of these certain things very early on.[19]

We see some of this in Abraham's family. After the incident where Abraham almost killed Isaac, which must have caused trauma, there were no further recorded conversations between Abraham and Isaac in the Bible, and the incident seems to have not been spoken of within the family ever again.

Second, families of potential future pathological liars can have contradictory standards regarding telling the truth. On the one hand, a child may be expected to tell their parents the truth about where they go and what they do. But, on the other hand, if the mother is hysterically crying again, or the parents are fighting again, the child is expected not to talk about it.[20]

Third, families where a child is disbelieved or not taken seriously if they report abuse by a family member to their parents can produce future pathological liars. Brushing aside a report of abuse from a child makes the child feel invalidated for having had the courage to tell the truth, thereby making that child less willing to tell their truth again.[21] Speaking ones truth is not welcome in these families.

Fourth, if a child feels punished for feeling certain emotions, the child can learn that expressing or feeling certain emotions is not permissible.[22] Sometimes children are punished for feeling angry at their parents, even without showing disrespect. Children are often discouraged from feeling sad. A child weeps and maybe is ridiculed by a parent who says something like, "Oh, stop being such a baby!" A child's emotions can be invalidated by their parents in this fashion.

And fifth, parents can set a bad example for their children when they witness their parents telling lies.[23] Children see when their parents tell lies to their neighbors, friends, extended family members, or even to each other. They see their parents lie in order to get out of an undesired situation. They see their parents lie in order to get what they want. They observe their parents lying, and learn to do the same.

A child can also lie to seek attention from an emotionally distant parent from whom they feel rejection.

The big problem is that the child who learned to lie as a coping mechanism for navigating their way through their dysfunctional family later becomes the inner child who controls the adult they have become. The inner child convinces their adult selves that the way to navigate their way through this confusing world, where lying is ostensibly frowned upon, but people are punished for telling the truth—is to lie, lie, lie.

***

I had a brother named Ishmael.[24] He was about 14 years old when I was born.[25] At some point, when I was old enough to understand such things, I learned that my brother Ishmael and I had the same father, but different mothers. My mother did not like Ishmael's mother or Ishmael.[26] My father asked Ishmael and his mother to leave our home.[27] I never saw Ishmael again until I was an adult. I thought that my parents treated my brother and his mother very unfairly.

One day, my father took some people and myself on a trip to make a burnt offering to God.[28] I noticed that my father was behaving a little strangely that day, like he was worried about something. On the way to the site of the burnt offering, I noticed that we didn't seem to have a sheep, ram, or any other animal for the offering.[29] *I told my father that I noticed this. I asked him about it. That made him even more worried. I could tell. He gave me some vague answer about how I should trust that God would provide what we needed for the sacrifice.*[30]

When we got to the site of the burnt offering, my father told me that God wanted him to put me on the altar and sacrifice me. That's right. I was to be a human sacrifice! I was so confused, to say the least. I mean, he said that God told him to do this. It was not in a voice that I could hear. But I didn't believe that my father would lie to me about something like that. But I was confused about why my father would want to kill me, and why God would want to kill me. None of this made sense.

Looking back, I felt shocked by the whole thing. I had no time to really think about it. So, as I remember, I just did as my father told me. I got up on the altar we had built. My father tied me up so that I couldn't move. There I was, ready to be killed and offered up as a sacrifice to God. It was terrifying! I felt alone—abandoned and betrayed by both my father, and by God.

I was confused as to why my father was doing this to me. Had I done anything wrong? Had I offended him for some reason? Did he blame me for the friction between my mother and Ishmael's mother? Did he hate me, and love Ishmael? After all, Ishmael was his eldest son really.

…I didn't know what to think.

Father tied me up and bound me to the altar. I opened my eyes briefly and got a quick glimpse of my father standing over me holding a big knife over his head with both hands, and aiming the knife directly at me.[31] *I closed my eyes and thought, "This is it." I braced myself for what was about to happen. I prayed and prayed for God to help me, hoping that God was not really behind all of this. I was as ready as I could be for my slaying by my own father, and then—and then—nothing. My father simply decided not to kill me.*[32]

To say that I was relieved would be an understatement.

My father saw a ram nearby, caught in a thornbush.[33] *I think he saw the ram as a sign from God that he was supposed to kill the ram instead of me. Later on, he would tell me that, just as he was about to kill me, he heard a voice from an angel above telling him to stop, and to kill the ram instead.*[34] *I did not hear that voice, but I'm glad my father heard it, or at least thought he heard it.*

My relationship with my father was not quite the same again after that whole incident. That incident haunted me for the rest of my life. How am I supposed to feel about that? My father, whom I'm supposed to trust more than anyone, tells me that he is supposed to kill me! Then he actually made plans to do it. He starts us on a journey with a lie—or at least a misleading half-truth about how we were just going to make a burnt offering to God— clearly giving the impression that he was going to sacrifice an animal. Was God okay with how my father lied to me like that?

After that whole incident, my relationship with my father chilled greatly. I mean, I didn't disavow him or anything. But we didn't really speak much about anything after that. In fact, I don't recall one meaningful conversation between the two of us after that at all.[35]

That whole incident messed me up.

***

Isaac married a woman named Rebekah. Together, they went on to have twin boys named Esau and Jacob. *Genesis 25:19-26.*

Isaac Blessing Jacob
Gerrit Willemsz Horst (1612-1652)

CHAPTER TEN

ISAAC & REBEKAH, JACOB & ESAU

"Lying lips are abomination to the LORD:
but they that deal truly are his delight"
                                        -- Proverbs 12:22

———

ISAAC AND HIS wife, Rebekah, had twin boys named Esau and Jacob. Each showed favoritism toward a different twin than the other. Isaac favored Esau, probably because Esau was the oldest and, therefore, the heir to the birthright as the eldest son. But Rebekah favored Jacob. *Genesis 25:28.* Rebekah's favoritism probably stemmed from God having told her, before the twins were born, that "the elder shall serve the younger," *Genesis 25:23*, meaning that Jacob would be superior to Esau even though Esau was the oldest. The Scripture says that "Isaac loved Esau" but "Rebekah loved Jacob," *Genesis 25:28*, implying that Esau was unloved by his mother, and Jacob was unloved by his father.

When a parent doesn't love a child, that right there is generational trauma just waiting to happen. Research shows that perceived parental favoritism negatively affects the mental health of all siblings, with harmful effects that persist long into adulthood.[1] We saw some of this in regard to Cain and Abel (see chapter 7).

It is clear from the Scriptures, though, that the whole family considered Esau to be irresponsible, lazy, and foolish. This is illustrated by a story in which Jacob swindles Esau out of his birthright by getting him to sell it to Jacob for a bowl of stew! *Genesis 25:29-33.* In the story, Jacob was making stew at home when Esau came in from somewhere, exhausted and hungry. Esau asked Jacob for some stew as he was very hungry. Jacob tells Esau, probably as a joke, that he would give him some stew if Esau agreed to sell him his birthright. Esau said, "Behold, I am at the point to die: and what profit shall this birthright do to me?" Jacob replied, "Sware to me this day." *Genesis 25:32-33.* Esau did what he was told and sold his birthright to Jacob. A very foolish deal to be sure.

Esau was probably seen as a "bad seed," especially to his mother, but maybe by both of his parents. Esau was probably traumatized by this. He must have felt rejected by his parents to a large degree. He engaged in at least one big passive-aggressive move by marrying outside the tribe. Esau and his wife Judith "were a grief of mind unto Isaac and to Rebekah." *Genesis 26:34-35.*

***

It came to pass that Isaac became very ill. *Genesis 27:1.* Isaac was old and blind. He thought he was about to die. *Genesis 27:7.* So Isaac called Esau, because he was the eldest son, and asked him to hunt some game, and make him a meal, which he could have for dinner, and bless Esau before Isaac died. *Genesis 27:3-4.* Isaac's intention was to pass down the blessing of the birthright to Esau as his firstborn son—meaning that Esau would then possess all of the rights of primogeniture.

Rebekah overheard the conversation between Isaac and Esau. *Genesis 27:5.*

Demonstrating blatant disdain for Esau, Rebekah came up with a scheme in which Jacob would lie to his blind father, by pretending to be Esau, thereby getting his father to bestow the irrevocable blessing granting Jacob, instead of Esau, the primogeniture rights under false pretenses. *Genesis 27:1-29.*

Rebekah's scheme was that Jacob would go and hunt for some game, she would prepare the meal, and then Jacob—pretending to be Esau—would go into Isaac's tent with the meal. *Genesis 27:8-13.* So that's what Jacob did. Jacob goes into the tent. Isaac, who could not

100

see, asked him who it was. Jacob said, "I am Esau, thy firstborn." *Genesis 27:19*. A blatant lie. Isaac suspected that he was Jacob when he said, "The voice is Jacob's voice." *Genesis 27:22*. So, Isaac asked him again, "Art thou my very son Esau?" *Genesis 27:24*. Jacob responded, "I am." Just—wow. Even after Isaac suspected something was wrong, and asked him a second time, Jacob bald-facedly lied again.

Isaac let go of any doubts he may have had, and just accepted that he was with Esau. He ate, drank wine, and probably exchanged some pleasantries and had some good conversation with his son, which he thought was Esau. Then Isaac gave Jacob—thinking he was Esau—an irrevocable blessing that was apparently binding even though given under false pretenses. *Genesis 27:27-28*. Then, Jacob went on his way.

Very shortly after this, Esau comes sauntering into Isaac's tent with *his* meal, as he was instructed by his father to do. *Genesis 27:30*. Both Esau and Isaac discover what Jacob had done. Isaac tells Esau that he gave his blessing to Jacob and that there was nothing he could do to reverse it or fix the situation. *Genesis 27:38-40*. Esau was now livid. He wanted to kill Jacob. *Genesis 27:41*. Realizing the danger that she had put Jacob in, Rebekah tells Jacob to hightail it out of town and go stay with her brother for a while. *Genesis 27:43*.

Interestingly, this story is told in the Scripture as if the previous story about Jacob swindling Esau out of his birthright for the stew never happened. *Genesis 25:32-33*.

It turns out that Isaac did not die during this whole incident. He went on to live a long life. After a long estrangement, Jacob and Esau put their differences aside and got together to bury their father. *Genesis 35:29*.

It should be noted that Scripture goes to great lengths to tell that, when it is said that God is the God of Abraham, and Isaac, and Jacob, Jacob's inclusion in that genealogical list was the result of a fraud. For some reason, the Bible author(s)—Moses?—wanted people to know that.

It is also worthy of note, that when the Bible refers to the God of these patriarchs, it refers to "the God of Abraham, and the God of Isaac, and the God of Jacob," *not* just the God of Abraham, Isaac, and

Jacob collectively. *Mark 12:26; Acts 7:32*; see also *Exodus 3:15*. Why? Because each of the three patriarchs had their *own* impression of God. It was not just one collective identical impression. Each of them, just as all individuals, had their own personal impressions of God.

***

I sensed very early on as a young boy that my mother didn't love me. It started as just a vibe. Then I began to see concrete evidence of her disdain for me. She clearly loved Jacob. She did not love me.

The truth is my whole family just sort of wrote me off almost from the start. Even though my father said I was his favorite—probably because I was his eldest son—I could tell that he still thought of me as kind of flighty and irresponsible. What can I say? I'm a free spirit of sorts. All of the strict rules about doing the chores, and then later doing my work and being responsible with the money and all of that, just seemed to make life miserable for me. I thought, 'Why can't I just be me?'

I didn't ask to be born. Why do I have to <u>become</u> anything? Why must I <u>do</u> something with my life? Why can't I enjoy life and do as I please? Is that so wrong?

My whole family, they think they're so holy or something. They think their lives are so meaningful. They're just going to die and be food for worms just like everybody else.

…They're not better than me.

The truth is, they're all full of it. All of them. Especially my brother, my twin. He has this holier than thou sanctimonious way about him. But then he goes and steals my birthright from me. Good man. He's really nothing but a swindler who lied to my blind father when he thought that he was on his death bed expressing his last wishes. What kills me is that everyone remembers him as the good one. The <u>good</u> twin. But in reality, he's the lying sack of … you know what. But he's the great Jacob—right? As in Abraham, Isaac, and Jacob. I don't see the greatness in any of the three of them, to be honest.

I admit it. I engaged in a lot of passive-aggressive behavior—as you call it today—toward my family, particularly my parents. I waited until I was over forty years old to get married. Then, I married <u>two</u> Canaanite women. Yeah, my parents hated that. They were seriously angry. I didn't care, though. Who are they to judge me? …Right?

Sometimes I remember getting the feeling that God loved Jacob, but hated me.[2] It was weird. It was like I could hear the voice of God within me saying, "Jacob I love, Esau I hate."[3] ...Really? ...Why? Why does God hate me? Have you ever asked yourself that question? Am I the only one? I'd bet not. I'd bet a lot of people ask themselves that question, at least once in a while.

It's a sad thing to go through life thinking that God hates you, or at least has no use for you. Am I part of God's plan? Does God have a plan for my life? For me? Am I just here to make my twin brother seem good by comparison? Ha! "Oh look! Jacob is so good, not like his loser brother, Esau."

I always felt like God—if there even is a God...there I said it— really didn't care about me at all. It feels like from the moment I was born, or even before that—like in my mother's womb—God had already decided that I was going to be a loser.[4] Does anything I'm saying make sense to you?

If I could pick just one word that describes my place in God's plan, that word would be abandoned. Like, maybe he doesn't hate me, maybe he doesn't love me. I sense abandonment and indifference from God, like he doesn't feel anything toward me one way or the other. Or he's not even really there. It's amazing how easy it is to feel so lost that you feel like your life does not matter.

***

The lack of love that Esau received from his mother, no doubt, affected him into his adulthood. Feeling unloved as a child can cause a whole slew of problems as an adult, including problems with closeness and intimacy, resulting in no deep meaningful relationships as an adult; undeveloped emotional intelligence; an impaired sense of self, leading to feelings of never being "good enough;" trust issues; difficulties navigating boundaries; codependency; fear of failure; feelings of isolation; extreme sensitivity; and general feelings of conflict and insecurity.[5]

***

In a classic example of reaping what one sows, *Galatians 6:7*, Jacob— who lied to his blind father in his old age—goes on to be mercilessly lied to by his own sons.

The generational trauma rolls on...

Joseph's Bloody Coat Brought to Jacob
Diego Velázquez (1599-1660)

CHAPTER ELEVEN

JACOB AND HIS SONS

"Even as I have seen, they that plow iniquity,
and sow wickedness, reap the same."
-- Job 4:8

———

A T HIS MOTHER'S behest, Jacob fled and remained away from home for many years, in fear for his life after having swindled Esau out of his birthright. *Genesis 27:43-45*. During that time, Jacob married and had many children. *Genesis 28-31*.

The day came when Jacob perceived that God had told him to return home and reconcile with Esau. *Genesis 32:3-12*. Jacob was afraid of Esau. He was not sure that Esau would accept his apology and gifts. *Genesis 32:11*. Because of this fear, Jacob sent his entire family on ahead to meet Esau first. Jacob trailed a day or two behind and camped by himself. *Genesis 32:24*.

While alone, he had an experience which Scripture describes as a wrestling match between Jacob and God. *Genesis 32:24-30*. Jacob expressed pride in the fact that he wrestled God face to face, and lived to tell about it. *Genesis 32:30*. At the end of the wrestling match, God tells Jacob, "Thy name shall be called no more Jacob, but Israel: for as a prince hast thou power with God and with men, and hast prevailed." *Genesis 32:28*.[1]

Are we supposed to interpret this event literally as if it were some sort of divine WWE match between God and Jacob? Or, is there more to it? Of course there's more to it. The very idea that an omniscient, omnipotent God literally engages in a wrestling match with a human being—and *loses* the match—is just plain ridiculous. What more likely occurred is that Jacob wrestled with his *impression* of God, like

105

Abraham before him in Genesis 18. Jacob perceived that God wanted him to reconcile with Esau. But what if his perception was wrong? What if Esau could not forgive him for stealing his birthright, and just killed him? Jacob was right to question his perception of God. It is foolish to just trust every voice in one's head that claims to be the voice of God. It could be just one's own imagination.

Abraham, Isaac, and Jacob were men who didn't blindly accept the impressions of God that were handed down to them—nor did they blindly accept their own impressions of God. They constantly questioned whether what they believed about God was true. They questioned whether the commands from God—which they thought they heard—were truly coming from God, or were just their imaginings. This is a healthy approach. Scripture tell us: "Beloved, believe not every spirit, but try the spirits whether they are of God." *1 John 4:1*. These patriarchs were doing this from day one. This is why Judaism is "a faith based on asking questions, sometimes deep and difficult ones that seem to shake the very foundations of faith itself."[2]

***

Jacob would go on to have twelve sons, one of the youngest of whom was Joseph. *Genesis 36:22-26*. Jacob openly showed favoritism toward Joseph. Joseph was clearly Jacob's favorite. For this reason, Joseph's brothers hated him. *Genesis 37:3-4*. Do you see the pattern here? Jacob's parents showed favoritism toward Jacob, causing all kinds of problems. Jacob went on to be a parent who also displayed favoritism toward one of his children.

Because of their hatred of Joseph—as a result of Jacob's favoritism—Joseph's brothers sold him into slavery. They went back and told Jacob that Joseph had been killed by a wild animal. They told this lie to Jacob, and let Jacob sob and mourn for his son right in front of them. *Genesis 37:18-35*. It was a very heartless thing to do. Do you see what happened here? Jacob heartlessly lied to his blind father. *Genesis 27:1,19*. In turn, Jacob's sons heartlessly lied to him. *Genesis 37:26-36*. This is how generational trauma works. Negative traits and tendencies are passed down to the descendants.

On the one hand, Scripture makes it clear that Abraham, Isaac, and Jacob had issues with the truth, especially regarding family matters. On the other hand, these three patriarchs are recognized by Jews and Christians alike as the founding fathers of God's people. God was still being referred to by the apostles of Jesus, some two thousand years later, as the God of Abraham, Isaac, and Jacob. *Acts 3:13.* This illustrates that forgiveness and mercy are available for people who do objectively wrong things as the result of their family inherited trauma.

Scripture teaches that there is mercy for those of us ensnared by this cycle of inherited generational trauma—which the Scripture simply refers to as sin—precisely because, through no fault of our own, we inherit the tendency to engage in maladaptive behavior, i.e., sin, from our parents, who in turn inherited it from *their* parents. And yes, we have personal responsibility for our actions. *Ezekiel 18:20.* But mercy is warranted because, as the saying goes: "You can't run away from your DNA."

***

I guess you could say that, in my family, lying was normalized. Since I was a child, it was clear to me that my parents have issues with the truth. I've witnessed both of them lying to other people, and lying to each other. They didn't lie every single day, or at least I think they didn't. But they lied often enough for me to notice it even at a young age.

On one occasion, my father made my mother lie in order to protect him. The incident happened on a trip they were on. My father made my mother lie and tell everyone that she was his sister and not his wife.³ I think he was scared that the men there would kill him and take my mother as their wife. He left my mother vulnerable to the advances of other men by giving them the impression that she was his unmarried sister. And the funny thing is, I heard that my grandfather did the same thing to my grandmother! ...Twice!⁴

Is it possible that lying runs in my family? ...I don't know.

Something happened to the way I viewed my parents after I'd seen them tell lies so often. It was disappointing to me. I can't explain it. Yes, I guess I became disappointed and disillusioned in them to a great extent. Isn't a child supposed to be able to trust their parents completely? But how can you completely trust people who lie like that so much? ...I don't know.

Maybe my dad inherited that lying habit from <u>his</u> parents. As I said, my grandfather lied about my grandmother being his sister just as my dad had done.

I heard my grandmother, Sarah, sometimes lied too. Maybe not big lies. But I heard she told lies that most would consider trivial. Like, I heard one story where she laughed about something, I guess she was embarrassed or ashamed to have laughed, then she just denied having laughed at all. She just flat out denied it.[5] Did you ever have someone laugh right in front of you, then a moment later they deny having laughed? Yeah, my grandmother did that.

But, I'm not one to judge because, you know what? I lie too.

I told a huge lie to my own father.[6] It was wrong. I know that now. I don't mean to shift the responsibility for what I did on someone else. But, the fact is, my mother pushed me to lie to my father.[7] You see, I had this brother, Esau, who was, shall we say, looked on as a bad seed by my whole family. I lied to him all the time. That was because I thought of him as foolish, irresponsible, and gullible. My parents viewed him the same way.

I was Mom's favorite. Esau was Dad's favorite, though. My mother questioned how my father could still prefer Esau over me knowing how much more responsible and reliable I was than him.

The day came when my father was very ill. He was blind, very sick, and thought he might die within days.[8] In fact, he eventually got better and lived for forty more years.[9] But, at the time, he thought his death was imminent.

My mother was very scared about my father dying. Not so much because she loved him or anything, because I don't think she really loved him. She was scared because, had my father died at that time, my brother Esau would inherit everything, as he was the eldest son. That would have made him the patriarch of our family. My mother would have had to rely completely on Esau to take care of her, and would have been beholden to him in her old age. Given her opinion of him as flighty and irresponsible, the prospect of relying on him for everything terrified my mother. So, to protect herself from indigency, she came up with a scheme.[10]

My mother encouraged me to steal my brother's birthright under false pretenses.[11] When my father told her that he wanted to see Esau in his tent so that he could give him the blessing of the birthright, Mom's scheme went into action. She told me to go into my father's tent and take advantage of the fact that he was blind by pretending to be Esau. She said that she took full responsibility for that whole deception.[12]

Apparently, my mother found out that the blessing of the birthright was irrevocable, even if given under false pretenses. The fact that she knew

108

that, led me to believe that this had been a plan of hers for some time.

I did exactly as my mother said. The plan worked. I got the birthright and everything that goes with that.[13] That's why, to this day, the lineage is Abraham, Isaac, and Jacob—not Abraham, Isaac, and Esau.

My brother hated me for swindling him. Who could blame him? I feared for my life as a result. My mother advised me to run. I think that was good advice. She thought I'd have to stay away for just a few days.[14] It turned out to be many years. I went on to get married while I was away and had children of my own.[15] I had twelve sons and a daughter.

After many years had passed, I felt that God wanted me to reconcile with my brother. I felt that God spoke this to me.[16] But, how could I be sure? I was scared. What if Esau just mercilessly killed me? What if he killed my family?

…What if I misheard God?

I wrestled with God on this one.[17] I needed to be sure that God was telling me the right thing to do or, rather, that I was really hearing from God, and hearing him right.

Can anyone ever really be sure that they're hearing from God, and hearing him right? …I don't know.

Anyway, thank God, Esau and I did reconcile and went on to have at least a cordial relationship. We peacefully got together to bury our father when he died.[18]

I deeply regret that I told my father an unconscionable lie.[19] My own sons went on to tell an unconscionable lie to <u>me</u>.[20] It's funny how that works. Right? We reap what we sow. Today you might say that whatever goes around, comes around. It's karma or poetic justice.

I also deeply regret showing blatant favoritism toward my son, Joseph, the way I did. That made his brothers hate him. They almost killed him. I should have known better. My mother's favoritism toward me—which was the motivation for her scheme for me to steal Esau's birthright—is what made Esau want to kill me. Favoritism from a parent can be devastating to the whole family. Wasn't the very first murder the result of God's favoritism toward Abel as opposed to Cain? Wasn't that what made Cain really hate Abel?[21] …Hmmm.

The rest of my sons resented the fact that I showed favoritism to my next to youngest son, Joseph. Looking back, yes, I probably brought on their resentment myself by doing so. I should have seen that coming. I should not have shown favoritism to Joseph so blatantly.

My sons initially came up with a plan to kill Joseph. Thankfully, they did not kill him.[22] However, they sold him into slavery, and then told me that he was killed by some wild animal. I sobbed and sobbed when they told me that news.[23] I thought Joseph was dead. My sons let me believe this until, as fate would have it, we were reunited with Joseph some twenty-two years later.[24] My sons robbed me of all that time with my beloved Joseph.

Did I deserve that? …Well, I did lie to my own father. It could be said that I reaped what I sowed. Did my sons learn to lie from me? Does something like that pass down through the blood?

All I know is that I learned a hard lesson.

***

Jacob had a cousin named Lot. *Genesis 11:27*. Lot, for some reason, traveled out of Ur and Haran with Abraham to the promised land. *Genesis 12:1-4*. Lot had two daughters. The story of Lot and his two daughters is probably *the* most glaring example of generational trauma in the entire Bible.

Lot and His Daughters
Artemisia Gentileschi (1593-1656)

CHAPTER TWELVE

LOT AND HIS DAUGHTERS

"Judah hath dealt treacherously,
and an abomination is committed in Israel and in Jerusalem."
-- Malachi 2:11

———

ABRAHAM HAD A nephew named Lot. *Genesis 12:5.* Lot wasn't a candidate for any father of the year awards either.

Just prior to the destruction of Sodom and Gomorrah, Lot offered hospitality to two angels and invited them to stay the night at his home in Sodom. *Genesis 19:1-3.* At some point during that evening, Lot's home was surrounded by men who demanded that Lot's two visitors come "out to us that we may have intimacies with them." *Genesis 19:5.* (This is precisely why certain sex acts were named after this town.) Lot came out of his house to plead with these men saying,

> I pray you, brethren, do not so wickedly. Behold now, I have two daughters which have not known man: let me, I pray you, bring them out unto you, and do ye to them as is good in your eyes: only unto these men do nothing: for therefore came they under the shadow of my roof.

Genesis 19:6-8. Wow. Strong was the family trauma in this one.

Were Lot's daughters traumatized by his parenting skills? Well, shortly after this incident in Sodom, both of Lot's daughters are said to have gotten Lot drunk—twice over two days—and both of them had sex with Lot without his knowledge, and both daughters got pregnant as a result of their sexual relations with their father. *Genesis 19:30-*

36.

Many people wonder why this story is in the Bible at all, including myself. What was the biblical narrative trying to convey? This story so offends the sensibilities of most that it is rarely, if ever, discussed in a church setting. I certainly don't remember any sermons or homilies on this.

Scripture seems to consistently point out very negative and unflattering things about even the greatest figures in the Bible. I can only chalk this up to the authors' intention to illustrate the pattern of inherited generational trauma which they were able to identify through their own inspired observations and discernment. While many are uncomfortable with this story, it is a story about familial trauma which the biblical authors deemed necessary to tell.

***

Trauma? You bet I had trauma. It's like I always say, sort of kidding around, that if you look in the dictionary under the word <u>trauma</u>, you'd see my picture! Ha! ...Alright, I stole that joke. But it's still pretty funny. ...No? I can joke about my trauma now.[1] But there really isn't anything funny about what happened to me at all.

I hope you appreciate this because this is <u>really</u> difficult for me to talk about. I dealt my whole life with sexual dysfunction like you wouldn't believe. I can't even bring myself to talk about most of it, even now after so much time. But I'll share parts of two stories with you. Maybe just one, depending on how difficult this is to talk about for me.

And I'm sharing these stories with you on the condition that you don't tell anyone my name. Just speak of me as Lot's daughter, that's it.

The times that I lived in were very bad for women in general, compared to the way things might be today. But, for myself and my sister, well, we had it very bad, even by the standards back then. And it was very bad for us primarily because of our father.

First of all, we lived in a town that was widely known for its ... sexual permissiveness, shall we say. My sisters and I all grew up there. My father chose to live there. I always wondered why that was so. We weren't particularly poor. In fact, we were very well off.[2] My father could have chosen to live wherever we wanted. I mean, there <u>were</u> better neighborhoods. But my father chose for us to live where we lived. As I grew, I began to realize that maybe

112

it was precisely because he wanted to be near the unseemly activity that was prevalent in our town.

I never really felt love from my father. There was an indifference there that I could not get past. I always had a feeling that I was abused sexually at some point as a very young child, probably by my father. Maybe things happened that were so horrific to me that I forgot them. Or, rather, chose not to remember them. Does that happen to people?[3] Are there people who suffer trauma that is so unimaginably horrible to them that they make themselves forget it? ...I don't know. But I had this haunting feeling for a long time that something must have happened to us, to my sister and to myself, because the both of us were seriously messed up.

And I always had this abiding feeling that there was a lot of "secret stuff" going on in his life that I would never know. ...I don't know. It was just a feeling.

Anyway, I have two stories to share.

One day, my father invited two men to visit us and stay the night.[4] The visit was going well enough when, just before it was time to go to bed, a group of men surrounded the house. It was scary. These men, however, seemed to know my father. And they knew we had company over, which I thought was odd.

So, this group of men yelled to my father from outside. They wanted him to bring our two visitors outside so that they could—for the lack of a better term—gang rape them.[5] I told you, that neighborhood was messed up, to say the least. I used to say we lived in "crazy town."

It gets worse.

So, my father goes outside and begs these men not to rape his guests.[6] But, get this. He begs them, "Please don't harm these men." Then he says, "I have two daughters. Take them and do what you want with them instead."[7]

I thought, "What?! Did I hear that right?! Did my father just offer up my sister and myself to be gang raped?!"

In that moment, I felt completely abandoned and betrayed by my father—and by the God that he and his uncle Abraham said they believed in.

But then, something odd happened. The group of men outside seemed all confused—all of a sudden. They were stumbling around like they were drunk and couldn't see straight. Then they all dispersed. No one got assaulted that day.

Did Abraham's God come to the rescue. …Who knows?

But my sister and I were scared out of our minds. We were scared that our father was so willing to offer us up like that, to be sexually assaulted by a group of men.

Is that enough trauma for you?

Then there's the time…

I want to be careful here. This is the first time I've ever shared this story outside of a very small circle of people.

There was one incident over a two-day period, when my sister and I… I'm sorry…

My sister and I got raped by our father.[8]

The story that got passed down in our family is that my sister and I got our father drunk, so that we could have our way with him.[9] That story was initiated by my father, probably as a preemptive strike in case we ever decided to tell our truth which, unfortunately, we never did.

Please. My sister and I got together and raped our father? Come on. We both got pregnant and…[10]

…I'm sorry. I really can't speak about this anymore. I'd like to stop now.

…Is that okay?

…Thank you.

***

Child sexual abuse is, without doubt, a major cause of family trauma and, therefore, a major cause of generational trauma as well. Child sexual abuse is underreported. So, the available statistics are probably lower than the reality. Statistics show that some 1 in 13 boys in the United States experience child sexual abuse, and as many as 1 in 4 girls do.[11] Experiencing child sexual abuse can affect how a person thinks, acts, and feels over a lifetime. Some of the long term mental and behavioral consequences victims of child sexual abuse can face include depression, post-traumatic stress disorder symptoms, and risky sexual behaviors.

According to Scripture, Abraham and Lot were called by God to leave their homeland and come to the land of Canaan. *Genesis 12:4.* Both of them came to Canaan together. Both of them brought a lot of inherited generational trauma with them—which they both passed on to their descendants.

***

The authors of Scripture wanted to make clear that inherited generational trauma was so prevalent, that no one was immune. Even the greatest prophet in the Old Testament—the Lawgiver himself—was not able to escape it.

Moses Before the Burning Bush
Sébastien Bourdon (1616-1671)

CHAPTER THIRTEEN

MOSES

"By faith Moses, when he was come to years,
refused to be called the son of Pharaoh's daughter."
-- Hebrews 11:24

———

MOSES WAS SOMEONE who, no doubt, experienced childhood trauma. His mother was forced to abandon him to be raised by the Egyptian royal family in order to save his life. Moses was raised by Pharaoh's daughter. It is clear however that, through a secret arrangement between Pharaoh's daughter and Moses's biological mother and sister, Moses was able to keep in touch with his biological mother as he grew up. *Exodus 2:1-10.*

As Moses grew, he learned that he was a Hebrew, and that his mother and sister were forced to be slaves in Egypt while he got to live like an Egyptian prince. This was certainly a source of trauma for Moses. On one occasion, after Moses became an adult, "he went out unto his brethren: and looked on their burdens." *Exodus 2:11.* He saw an Egyptian beating one of his fellow Hebrews. Moses was so incensed by this, that he killed the Egyptian right there on the spot and hid his body. *Exodus 2:12.*

***

I already put together five books in which I gave my account of the things that transpired between God and myself. Some people did some editing of my work after me. But I think it's all still fairly accurate. However, I can share some things that were not emphasized enough in my writings.

My story begins with the actions of some very courageous women to whom I owed my very life.

I was born during the reign of Seti the First, the Pharaoh, the king of Egypt.[1] At the time of his reign, my people the Israelites had been slaves in Egypt for over four hundred years. Seti became afraid of the Israelites because he felt that they—that is we—were becoming too numerous. I guess he was afraid of a slave revolt. He ordered that all of the male babies born to the Israelite women be killed immediately after birth. He ordered the Israelite midwives to carry out his murderous deed.[2]

The Israelite midwives, however, got together and defied the orders of the Pharaoh even though it might have led to their imprisonment or execution.[3] I am indebted to all of the midwives, especially the ones who helped my birth mother in her time of need.

I was raised by two mothers. No, they were not a couple. My birth mother was named Jochebed. She had a sad story herself. She had to give me up for adoption as an infant. My adoptive mother was named Bithiah.[4] My adoptive mother was the daughter of the Pharaoh.

These two women should be household names. The both of them, together, put their own lives in peril in order to save mine. I owed them everything. Those two were more courageous than any men I knew. My adoptive mother, Bithiah, knew full well of her father's edict that all of the Hebrew baby boys be killed upon birth. But she had a conscience. She was a woman of courage and conviction. She defied her father's orders knowing that the consequences, if she were to be caught, would be dire.

Bithiah also had an understanding with my birth mother, Jochebed. She showed my birth mother great compassion by first allowing her to nurse me as an infant, and then allowing my blood family and I to keep in touch throughout my childhood.[5]

I never forgot how much I owed these women for what they had done for me. I remembered them when, one day, during our wandering in the wilderness days, five women came to me and told me that their father had died.[6] These women had no brothers. And according to the law at the time, if a man had no sons, only daughters, the daughters would not get any inheritance from their father but, rather, the father's brother would get all of his inheritance. The women's uncle would get their father's inheritance, not them. The women would be left with nothing.

The five women who pleaded with me thought that this law was unfair. I did too. So, after praying about it, I changed the law so that women could inherit their father's estate, if their father had no sons.[7] I did that. I was proud of having done that. I learned respect for strong women at a very early age. I know, people think of me as an old-fashioned patriarchal figure— perhaps even a misogynist. But what I did with that law right there was a big step in the right direction, I think. Wasn't I way ahead of my time with regards to women's rights?

And, speaking of strong women, let's not forget my sister, Miriam, who was actually a prophet of God at a time when women weren't typically accepted as such.[8] I never told her this, but she was one of my role models. I think she would have done a better job than me of confronting Pharaoh about freeing the Israelites from slavery, if given the chance. Except that women were not taken seriously as leaders back then. So, Pharaoh probably would not have even given her an audience.

As I grew, I became very conflicted about the fact that my birth mother, my brother Aaron, my sister Miriam, and all of our people were slaves in Egypt while I got to grow up with Egyptian royalty. My Egyptian mother saw to it that my birth mother and her family were looked after and treated well. When I got old enough, I took on that responsibility. But the truth is, I liked living the life of an Egyptian prince. Who wouldn't? For most of my youth, I identified as Egyptian.[9] When I was younger, I looked down on slaves. I considered myself superior to them and deserving of all the trappings of wealth and power that I possessed. I tried to suppress the fact that I was a Hebrew. I tried not to think about it. But there was always that part of my conscience that didn't let me forget where I came from. When I became and adult, I came to terms with the fact that—as much as I loved and was grateful to Bithiah for everything she had done for me—I was not Bithiah's son. I didn't belong with her and her people. I was a Hebrew—a descendant of slaves. …That's who I was.

This inner conflict within me about who I was came to a head when I ventured out, one day, to Goshen to investigate for myself the toil of the slavery of my fellow Hebrews.[10] There I was, in all of my royal Egyptian garb, feeling all high and mighty like a slave-master checking out the opera- tions. But, of course, I knew I was a Hebrew and that, by rights under Egyptian law at the time, I belonged laboring and toiling right there along- side the rest of the Hebrews. …I felt like such an imposter!

I was overwhelmed with guilt. I thought of myself as one of them. Per- haps for the very first time, I began to empathize with their plight. I wanted to help them. I wanted to stand up and proudly declare to them all, "I am a Hebrew!!" …But I was too much of a coward to do that. Revealing myself as a Hebrew would have meant I'd have to be a slave myself. And there would probably be extra punishment for having gotten away with posing as an Egyptian prince for so long. Plus, I didn't want to get my Egyptian mother in any kind of trouble. My lifelong façade of being an Egyptian was really thanks to her doing.

When I saw an Egyptian beating a Hebrew slave, that was too much for me at that moment. It was like, all of a sudden, while watching that Egyptian man beat the Hebrew slave, to me he was beating my mother and my brother and my sister. He was beating all of my people. He was beating me.

Then, in a blind rage. I killed him.[11]

I killed him, and I hid the body.

Then, I went home.

I got away with it—or so I thought.

The next day, I went out to Goshen again. I saw two Hebrews fighting. I tried to break up the fight. One of the Hebrews asked me who I thought I was telling them what to do. Then he asked me if I was going to kill him like I had killed the Egyptian man the previous day.[12]

I was shocked! I was so sure nobody saw.

Fear and dread overcame me.

"What do I do now?" I thought.

I knew I had to flee. I heard that Pharaoh wanted to execute me for killing the Egyptian.

So, I fled. I ran to Midian.[13]

As I arrived in Midian, I met a woman I would marry. Her name was Zipporah. I married her and had children with her. I lived a long fruitful life with her. I remained away from Egypt until I was very elderly.

I had become a fugitive. Because of this, I continued to feel like a coward. I continued to live a lie. Except now, instead of pretending to be an Egyptian prince, I was pretending to be a man who was not wanted for murder. I just went from one façade to another.

I lived my life employed as a shepherd for my father-in-law. At some point during my days in Midian, the Pharaoh, Seti I, who had sentenced me to death,[14] had passed away.[15]

During my last days as a fugitive shepherd, I felt that God was calling me—speaking to me.[16] I saw this weird bush that seemed to be on fire, but yet was not being consumed or burning.[17] Ironically, people who read my account of what happened often refer to this as the story of the burning bush.

Moses

But, the whole point of the miracle I saw was that the bush was <u>not</u> burning. I made that very clear. I don't get people sometimes.

I thought it was odd that God chose me to be his spokesman. I had a speech impediment, a stutter, all my life.[18] Shouldn't the ability to speak be a critical criterion for a job as God's spokesperson? …I don't know.

God told me that he wanted me to demand that Pharaoh free all of the Hebrew slaves. But he also told me that he would harden Pharaoh's heart to make him obstinately refuse to let the Hebrews go.[19] Right there, I have to admit, I got a little concerned. God tells me to demand that Pharaoh free the slaves—and then he's going to basically tell Pharaoh not to do it. My big fear was that God was setting me up for failure in that he was going to abandon me in my time of need before Pharaoh by making me look like an old fool.[20]

Since I stuttered, my brother Aaron came with me whenever I spoke to the Pharaoh. I would speak the words to Aaron, and then he would relay what I said to Pharaoh.[21]

The first time I went to speak to the Pharaoh was scary. I told Pharaoh what God told me to say. It just made him angry. As a result of what I did, he made the working conditions of the Hebrew slaves even more difficult.[22] The Israelite foremen were none too pleased with me. They blamed me for making matters worse for them and said that God should punish me for what I did.[23] I remember thinking, "See? God set me up to look like a fool!" I confronted God with how I felt. I asked him why he was treating the Hebrew slaves so badly, and why he sent <u>me</u>, of all people, on this mission. And why, after more than four hundred years of slavery, he had done <u>nothing</u> to rescue them.[24] That's right, I said all that. God responded by telling me to have patience, and to wait and see what he was going to do.[25]

Wait and see. Wait and see.

God sent me back to Egypt. One day, soon after I arrived with my wife in Egypt, I had a very strong feeling that God wanted to kill me![26] I know, it sounds crazy. But that's how I felt. I think it was because I had neglected to circumcise my son, Gershom.[27] You might think of me as paranoid or overly suspicious. But I thought that God was out to get me. I thought that he had a plan to kill me and then make it look like it was my fault— like I did something to make it seem as if I deserved to die. And then people would say, "Poor Moses. He got what was coming to him, though." Because God would be above suspicion. No one would have the courage to say that God killed me unjustly.

121

Regarding my relationship with my family, I had a big wake up call. One day, I learned that my own brother Aaron, and my own sister Miriam, thought of me as an arrogant, egotistical, autocrat. The two of them actually went before all of the people, during our wandering in the wilderness days, and said that God didn't just speak through me, God spoke through them too, they said. They thought I had too much power. They wanted to share power with me.[28] I had accepted the fact that many of the Israelites in the desert were grumbling and complaining. But these two were my close blood family.

Were they jealous of me all along? They said that God spoke to them same as he had spoken to me.[29] They asked why they shouldn't be leaders of the people same as me. Honestly, I didn't have an answer for that. I told you that, in my sister's case, I think she would have been a better spokesperson and leader than me. After all, she helped to save my life when I was an infant.[30] She was just a child herself at the time. She displayed great courage for someone so young.

I certainly was not a perfect man. I think God had reason to be angry and disappointed with me. God was right not to let me be the one to lead the people into the promised land.[31] I didn't feel like I was worthy of such an honor.[32]

***

It is interesting to note here that the tenth and final plague—which eventually led to the freeing of the Israelites—was the death of every firstborn son in Egypt, including Pharaoh's son. *Exodus 11:1-8.* That punishment was mass infliction of family trauma.

Moses experienced familial trauma, and left much familial trauma in his wake.

CHAPTER FOURTEEN

KING DAVID

"Have mercy upon me, O God, according to thy lovingkindness: according unto the multitude of thy tender mercies blot out my transgressions. Wash me throughly from mine iniquity, and cleanse me from my sin. For I acknowledge my transgressions: and my sin is ever before me. Against thee, thee only, have I sinned, and done this evil in thy sight: that thou mightest be justified when thou speakest, and be clear when thou judgest."
-- Psalm 51:1-4

———

NOTHING IS RECORDED in the Bible about David's earliest childhood years. In some midrashic traditions, David was born out of wedlock. His mother is said to be named Nitzevet.[1] His father is known from Scripture as Jesse. *Ruth 4:17.* Tradition holds that one of his parents was his biological parent, but it is unclear who. Tradition leans heavily in favor of his father Jesse being his biological father.

Scripture calls David the root of Jesse. *Isaiah 11:10.* St. Paul of Tarsus interpreted Isaiah's reference to the root of Jesse as a foreshadow referring to Jesus Christ. *Romans 15:12.*

Proponents of the theory that David was born out of wedlock point to Psalm 51, which tradition says was authored by David. It says: "Behold, I was shapen in iniquity, and in sin did my mother conceive me." *Psalm 51:5.* Tradition has it that King David wrote this penitential psalm shortly after the prophet Nathan came to him and told him that God was angry with him for having had an adulterous affair with a woman named Bathsheba, and murdering her husband, Uriah, in an attempt to cover up the affair. *2 Samuel 12:1-15.*

***

David's story begins in Scripture when God sends a prophet named Samuel to David's home so that Samuel could anoint David as the next king of Israel. *1 Samuel 16:1-13*. David's father, Jesse, had eight sons, the youngest of whom was David. When Samuel asked Jesse if he could see his sons, "Jesse made seven of his sons to pass before Samuel." *1 Samuel 16:10*.

Samuel asks Jesse if these seven were all of his sons. Jesse then unenthusiastically tells him that he had one more son—which was David—but that he was outside tending sheep. Jesse didn't even offer to call David and bring him in for Samuel to see. Samuel had to insist on seeing David saying "we will not sit down till he come hither."*1 Samuel 16:11*. This clearly suggests that, for some reason, Jesse was embarrassed of David, or at least not very proud of him.

A case of disfavored treatment of a child by a parent, rears its ugly head once again.

There's no way a child grows up and doesn't realize that his father is ashamed of him. Without even knowing the details of why Jesse was ashamed of David—or what transpired between this father and his son—we can safely infer that this one incident with Samuel the prophet points directly to a potentially trauma causing problem.

***

While nothing is really known about David's upbringing, it *is* known that David, as a father, had much familial trauma in his *own* family. David is said to have had some twenty children altogether, with his many wives. *1 Chronicles 3:1-9*. David's firstborn son was Amnon. Amnon raped Tamar, his sister. *2 Samuel 13:1-14*. David's third son was Absalom. Absalom had Amnon killed. *2 Samuel 13:28-29*. Absalom turned against his father, David, and actually turned the hearts of the people of Israel against him. Absalom instigated a conspiracy against David. *2 Samuel 15:7-12*. This was definitely not one big happy family, to say the least.

Absalom's conspiracy against his father spiraled into a civil war. Scripture tells us that a man named Shimei cursed David to his face calling him "a bloody man" while throwing rocks at him. *2 Samuel 16:8,13*. David had to flee Jerusalem for his own safety. David's army fought against Absalom's army. But being Absalom's father, David commanded his army to deal gently with Absalom, meaning he didn't want him killed. *2 Samuel 18:5*. But Joab, a leader in David's army, out of a sense of loyalty to David, killed Absalom when he had the chance, disregarding David's order to deal gently with him. *2 Samuel 18:14*.

Note, though, that David did indeed have a reputation among many of being "a bloody man."

***

Even though David had a reputation of being "a bloody man," took a man's wife, committed adultery with her many times, and then killed the man so that he could marry her, David was referred to in Scripture as someone whose heart was "perfect with the LORD his God," *1 Kings 11:4*, and as a man after God's own heart, *1 Samuel 13:14; Acts 13:22*. That's some good PR right there.

Solomon, the fourth son of David and his wife Bathsheba, was chosen by David to succeed him as king. *1 Kings 1:30,38-39*. David said that God told him that Solomon was to build the Temple for God instead of him because he was "a man of war, and hast shed blood." *1 Chronicles 28:3*. According to David, God told him, "Solomon thy son, he shall build my house and my courts: for I have chosen him to be my son, and I will be his father." *1 Chronicles 28:6*.

David died, and Solomon succeeded him as king. *1 Kings 2:10-12*. During Solomon's reign, God became angry with him "because his heart was turned from the LORD God of Israel." *1 Kings 11:9*. Solomon "had seven hundred wives, princesses, and three hundred concubines: and his wives turned away his heart." *1 Kings 11:3*. Solomon's wives are said to have "turned away his heart after other gods." *1 Kings 11:4*. Yet, Scripture characterizes Solomon as the wisest man in the world. *1 Kings 4:30-31*. I wonder if he hired the same PR firm as his father, David.

***

As far back as I can remember, I had this abiding sense that my family didn't like me.[2] I think my mother loved me. But I always felt that my father and my brothers hated me. I got the sense that they made me be a shepherd because they wanted me out of the house as much as possible. They also sent me on a lot of errands. I thought that they secretly hoped that I would be attacked and killed by a wild animal while I was outdoors for so long with no one to protect me. I spent a lot of time alone outdoors.

Spending so much time alone gave me time to reflect and pray. …Yes, I prayed. I prayed to God because I felt like I had no one else. I felt so unloved and unwanted. During my alone time, I taught myself how to play musical string instruments. I became widely recognized for my skills at playing music on the harp and lyre.[3]

I felt rejected and unloved by my parents.[4] I hoped for acceptance from God. I felt fatherless. I began to see God as my father. I hoped that God would want to be a father to the fatherless.[5]

I enjoyed playing music. I started making up songs when I was very young. I poured my heart and soul into my songs. My songs were mostly about how I felt about life, and how I felt about God. Depending on my mood, sometimes I praised and worshipped God, sometimes I pleaded with God for mercy, forgiveness, or protection, and sometimes, yes, I complained to God about various things.

It bothered me that my brothers and my father thought of me as a loser. I wanted to show them otherwise. I remember constantly thinking, "I'm not a loser!!" I grew so tired of being disrespected and underestimated. One of my most satisfying moments was when I killed that giant named Goliath. Oh, man![6]

I was out on one of those errands that my father sent me on.[7] My brothers were out on a battlefield fighting these people called the Philistines. They were a tribe that was hostile to the people of Israel. My brothers were all soldiers in this war against the Philistines. My father sent me to the battlefield to see what was happening and to bring back news to him about my brothers.[8] My father saw me as this loser kid who wasn't old enough, big enough, or brave enough to fight. Despite the fact that I was chosen by a prophet to be the next king of Israel, I think my father was still embarrassed to call me his son. All I was good for was relaying news to him from the front lines.

While there, I saw this Philistine, Goliath, taunting all of these men in our army.[9] It was embarrassing! He was challenging them to send someone to fight him one on one. No one was brave enough to take him on. I don't know where I found the courage to accept his challenge.[10] That courage must have come straight from God. I had someone watch my carriage, and told Goliath I'd fight him.[11] Then, Goliath laughed at me and mocked me.[12] I hated that. It was the disrespect and underestimation. It just made me want to beat him even more.

What he didn't realize is that all of those years being sent outside to watch our sheep worked to my advantage. You see, I became rather skilled with the slingshot because that's how I chased the wolves away from our sheep.[13] I practiced using the slingshot for hours at a time on most days. I used to aim at trees, bushes, boulders, you name it. I got so skilled that I began to hit wolves all the time. So, after I accepted the challenge to fight Goliath, my weapon of choice was a slingshot.[14] That evoked more laughter. Goliath openly mocked my choice of weapon. He also mocked the fact that, even though these men found the smallest suit of armor they could find, it was still too big for me.[15] I must have looked ridiculous in that ill-fitting suit with a slingshot as a weapon. I just took the suit off.[16]

I found a good-sized stone for my slingshot. I put the stone in my sling-shot pouch. I tried to look as confident as I could, even though I was scared out of my mind. I spun the stone around in a big circle with my right arm. I said a quick prayer to God, asking him to help me do this. I made a mental count of three, "One...two...three!" I released the stone from the slingshot. Then...bam!! I thought I hit him.[17] Then I knew I did hit him. Then, after a brief pause, he fell to the ground. I remember thinking, "Is he unconscious?" He was just laying there. I realized I had hit him right be-tween the eyes.[18] Right between the eyes through a small slit in his armored helmet. That was so awesome! It was such a rush! I began to look for another stone for when he regained consciousness.[19] But he wasn't awakening. Some of the other Philistines went to check on Goliath. Then they realized that he was dead, and ran off all scared. Ha! I remember thinking, "Yeah, that's right! You better run!"[20] Then the crowd of my people began chanting my name. I was a big hero! I remember wishing that my father had been there to see that.

I thought to myself, "See, Dad? I'm not a loser!"

...I can't believe I just said that.

...Did I spend the rest of my life trying to prove to my father again and again that I'm not a loser?

...I wasn't perfect. I never claimed to be so. As someone famously said, "I never said I was a role model."

I've had many regrets.

I don't know if I'm worthy of being remembered as someone with a heart after God. But I am honored to be thought of that way.

***

73 of the 150 psalms in the Bible have headings attributing them to David.[21] If these attributions are historically accurate, then we have a treasure trove of writings from David which give us a look, or perhaps just a glimpse, into his mind and his heart and his relationship with his God. We have many of his own prayers, thoughts, and reflections right there in the Bible.

David's psalms reveal a man who deeply desired a relationship with God, but also struggled in that endeavor. His psalms range from praising and worshipping God, to begging God for help, to expressions of gratitude for God's help, to complaining about why God wasn't helping him.

One of David's lowest points, no doubt, was when he asked God: "My God, my God, why hast thou forsaken me?" *Psalm 22:1*. At the time, David felt abandoned by God. He was certainly not alone among the people of the Bible in feeling and expressing that sentiment. Feelings of abandonment, rejection, and betrayal from God permeate Scripture from beginning to end. Jesus would go on to famously quote David's psalm while on the Cross—feeling abandoned, rejected and betrayed by God too. *Matthew 27:46; Mark 15:34*.

***

The first of the Four Noble Truths of Buddhism is that suffering is universal.[22] There is no escaping it. Everyone suffers to one degree or another. Everyone.

Buddhism teaches that most suffering is in our minds, i.e., we experience trauma. We suffer because we want what we can't have, and we can't have what we want. We want our lives to go a certain way and, except in rare instances, it doesn't.[23] We may experience exciting moments and times. But are we happy? Do we have joy?

Similarly, Scripture makes it clear that inherited generational trauma has been around since the beginning. It affects how we see and experience life. It affects how we see and experience God.

No one escapes the pain of generational trauma in this world. And I mean no one.

What could be more traumatic than being crucified?

CHAPTER FIFTEEN

JESUS

"But whom say ye that I am?"
-- Matthew 16:15

———

THE LIFE OF Jesus has been described as the greatest story ever told. The famous poem *One Solitary Life* correctly points out that—even though Jesus was the "child of a peasant" and that he was "born in an obscure village," "never wrote a book" or "went to college"…etc.—today, Jesus "is the central figure of the human race."

Shortly after he had been baptized—and then spent 40 days in the desert being tested by the devil—Jesus came back to Nazareth and began teaching in the local synagogues throughout Galilee. He became well known and respected doing this. *Luke 4:14*. Jesus regularly read from Scripture at his local synagogue in Nazareth. *Luke 4:16*.

On one Sabbath, he stood up to read, and was handed the book of Isaiah. *Luke 4:17*. Jesus took this opportunity to announce his mission and purpose. This actually did not go so well. Jesus looked for the passage that he wanted to read in the scroll that was handed to him—and read.[1]

> The Spirit of the Lord is upon me, because he hath anointed me to preach the gospel to the poor; he hath sent me to heal the brokenhearted, to preach deliverance to the captives, and recovering of sight to the blind, to set at liberty them that are bruised, To preach the acceptable year of the Lord.

Luke 4:18-19. So far, so good. However, Jesus went on to say something which enraged the entire congregation. He said, "This day is this scripture fulfilled in your ears." *Luke 4:21.* He essentially told everyone that he was the Messiah that Isaiah predicted. That *he* was going to be the one to preach to the poor, heal the brokenhearted, preach deliverance...etc. His messianic claim alone was enough to ruffle some feathers. But what really caused Jesus some problems that day was that he said that *he* needed to do all of these things, because the religious leaders of his day—and those that led before them—had failed miserably at this mission for many generations. *Luke 4:25-27.*

To say that Jesus irked these people would be a gross understatement. Scripture tells us that "when they heard these things," they "were filled with wrath." *Luke 4:28.*

Jesus reminded them that, from day one, among the very people who considered themselves God's own, there were always many who were poor and brokenhearted—who felt oppressed. They felt abandoned, betrayed, and rejected by the very God they were told to obey, worship, and serve. They went through things that they thought God would protect them from. And through it all, they looked helplessly toward God in heaven and cried, "Why?!"

"Wherefore hast thou afflicted thy servant?" *Numbers 11:11.*

"Why came we forth out of Egypt?" *Numbers 11:20.*

"Alas, O Lord GOD, wherefore hast thou at all brought this people over Jordan, to deliver us into the hand of the Amorites, to destroy us?" *Joshua 7:7.*

"Wherefore hath the LORD smitten us to day before the Philistines?" *1 Samuel 4:3.*

"Why hast thou set me as a mark against thee?" *Job 7:20.*

"Why standest thou afar off, O LORD? why hidest thou thyself in times of trouble?" *Psalm 10:1.*

"How long wilt thou forget me, O LORD? forever? how long wilt thou hide thy face from me?" *Psalm 13:1.*

"Lord, how long wilt thou look on?" *Psalm 35:17.*

"How long, LORD? wilt thou be angry for ever? shall thy jealousy burn like fire?" *Psalm 79:5.*

"How long, LORD? wilt thou hide thyself for ever? shall thy wrath burn like fire?" *Psalm 89:46.*

"LORD, how long shall the wicked, how long shall the wicked triumph?" *Psalm 94:3.*

"O LORD, why hast thou made us to err from thy ways, and hardened our heart from thy fear?" *Isaiah 63:17.*

"Wherefore hath the LORD pronounced all this great evil against us?" *Jeremiah 16:10.*

"O LORD, how long shall I cry, and thou wilt not hear!" *Habakkuk 1:2.*

***

Scripture says that when Jesus was born, God "was made flesh, and dwelt among us." *John 1:14.* This is known as the doctrine of the Incarnation.[2] The Church teaches that Jesus was both fully human and fully Divine. He was not part God and part human. Whatever else Christians may believe about the divinity of Jesus, it is important to remember that he was a flesh-and-blood human being the same as you and I. If you think about it, it can seem ridiculous that this needs to be pointed out. But it does. Jesus was a human being. As such, he was subject to all of the limitations that we refer to as the human condition.

Jesus had a psychological makeup. Of course he did. If he didn't, he wouldn't have been truly human. But he *was* human. He was therefore subject to whatever psychological trauma his genetics and environment threw his way.

As a matter of doctrine, though, Jesus never sinned. *1 Peter 2:22; Hebrews 4:15.* This is entirely plausible if we understand this to mean that Jesus never committed mortal sin, i.e., sin that threatens to sever our relationship with God—serious, willful violations of the Ten Commandments.[3] But does this mean that Jesus was a perfect human being who never committed any kind of *faux pas*? Jesus never made mistakes? Jesus didn't have any kind of personal flaws? Jesus never did anything he later regretted? Scripture doesn't assert any of these things. Scripture simply says that Jesus never sinned. I can accept that. But all humans have imperfections that do not necessarily rise to the level of serious sin. To be human is to be imperfect.[4]

I therefore respectfully submit that Jesus *must* have had *some* imperfections. The term perfect human being can be said to be an oxymoron—no such thing. Jesus did ask us, in the Sermon on the Mount, to aim for perfection. *Matthew 5:48.* However, I think that this is an ideal for which we are asked to strive. I don't think any human being can actually live a perfect life.

Scripture does not say that Jesus was always perfect. It says that he was *made* perfect through the things that he suffered. *Hebrews 2:10*. This means he was not perfected until his suffering and death on the Cross. But while he lived, he grew in age and wisdom. *Luke 2:52*. In order to be *made perfect*, he must have been imperfect prior to that.

We can still accept that Jesus lived a sinless life, if we so choose, even if we believe that Jesus—because he was human—must have had some imperfections. For example, he could have been flawed in any number of ways. Hypothetically, he could have had personality flaws. He could have had an annoying personality. He could have made other people uncomfortable. None of this would rise to the level of serious sin—but they might very well be imperfections or flaws. Did Jesus ever do things that might be described as imperfect?

Jesus did do several things that many might find offensive today. For example, Jesus once got angry at a fig tree because he was hungry and he looked for fruit on the tree, and found nothing but leaves. So, he killed the tree because he found no figs on it to eat. He wished the tree dead. The tree immediately withered away. *Matthew 21:18-20*. He killed the tree for not bearing fruit, even though it was "not the time of figs." *Mark 11:13*. (Come on, cut the tree a break. It wasn't the season for figs!) Then, Jesus told his disciples who witnessed him kill the tree that if they had faith, they would be able to will death to a fig tree too. *Matthew 21:21*. Many environmentalist-minded individuals would consider this action sinful. Killing a tree simply because it was not bearing fruit—even though it was not even the season for that fruit—seems a bit unjust. It also might be indicative of an anger issue.

Now, you might argue that it is unfair to judge Jesus's actions here by today's standards. People weren't as environmentally conscious back then as they are today. Killing a tree for no good reason was not seen as a bad or sinful thing back then. But, are you not then saying that Jesus was a man of his time? That he was behaving as a human being of his day, without any 21st century ecological values? In other words, a normal human being with a 1st century worldview.

In another incident, Jesus performed one of his many exorcisms and cast some demons out of a man who was possessed by them. *Mark 5:1-13*. After they left the man, the demons asked Jesus for permission to enter a nearby herd of swine instead. The Scripture tells us that

> forthwith Jesus gave them leave. And the unclean spirits went out, and entered into the swine: and the herd ran violently down a steep place into the sea, (there were about two thousand;) and were choked in the sea.

Mark 5:13. Killing two thousand innocent pigs surely offends the sensibilities of animal lovers today. Of course, this incident must be considered in light of the fact that, in Judaism, pigs are considered to be filthy animals. To most people, this would be akin to Jesus killing 2,000 rats. Not too many tears would have been shed for the rats.

There was a time when Jesus appeared to tell a lie to members of his own family.[5] This occurred during one particular year just before the Jewish Feast of Tabernacles (Sukkot). *John 7:2*. Jesus's brothers told him to go to Judea "that thy disciples also may see the works that thou doest." *John 7:3*.[6] Notably, Jesus's own brothers did not believe in him. *John 7:5*. Jesus, possibly sensing a trap set up by his brothers, told them to go to the feast without him because he was not going to go. *John 7:8*. So, his brothers went without him. But as soon as Jesus's brothers left, "then went he also up unto the feast, not openly, but as it were in secret." *John 7:10*. It clearly appears here that Jesus did not tell his brothers the truth. Jesus was therefore not above telling a lie in certain situations.

Did Jesus sin by telling his brothers a lie? The Church teaches that "[t]he gravity of a lie is measured against the nature of the truth it deforms, the circumstances, the intentions of the one who lies, and the harm suffered by its victims."[7] In order for a lie to rise to the level of serious or "mortal" sin, it must do "grave injury to the virtues of justice and charity."[8] Jesus told his brothers—whom Jesus probably did not trust because they did not believe in him—that he wasn't going to the feast. Was there any grave injury here? It doesn't seem that way to me. Was it wrong for Jesus to mislead them? Maybe. Perhaps I'm wrong to suggest that Jesus lied. But, let's be honest, what Jesus told his brothers, in this instance, was not the truth.

I question why this story is even in the Scripture. Whoever decided to put it in there had to know that it might cast aspersions on Jesus's integrity, at least for some. Or maybe they just wanted to show that no one is perfect—not even Jesus.

Many people cite some of the things that Jesus said as being flat out antisemitic.[9] One of such statements was about a man named Nathanael who was curious about what he had heard about Jesus, and came to visit him. When he saw Nathanael approaching, Jesus said, "Behold an Israelite indeed, in whom there is no guile!" *John 1:47*. The idea that Jesus would express surprise at finding a guileless Israelite offends many people. It is uncertain what Jesus may have meant by this. I don't think Jesus intended to be antisemitic, being that Jesus was Jewish himself.

The Gospel of John, in particular, has been cited by many as having an antisemitic streak throughout. This includes having Jesus say seemingly antisemitic things himself. This is a very different take on Jesus than is found in the other three Gospels—known among Bible scholars as the Synoptic Gospels. For example, in the other three Gospels, whenever Jesus had discussions with Jewish leaders, the people Jesus argued with were specifically described as either Pharisees, Sadducees, Scribes...etc. In the Gospel of John, when Jesus argued with those same people, and those people said or did something, the Gospel simply refers to them as "the Jews."[10] And the Gospel of John particularly emphasizes that "the Jews" sought to kill Jesus. *John 5:18; 7:1; 10:24,31.*

The writers/editors of the Gospel of John repeatedly referred to "the Jews" when they should have referred to *some* of the religious leaders back then.

In another incident, a gentile woman came to Jesus for help because her daughter was demon-possessed. She said, "Have mercy on me, O Lord, thou Son of David, my daughter is grievously vexed with a devil." *Matthew 15:22*. She addressed Jesus as "Lord" and "Son of David." Despite this, Jesus initially responded to this woman by ignoring her, and not saying a word to her. *Matthew 15:23*. This alone comes across as a bit rude. Some of Jesus's disciples asked him to send her away because she kept bothering them with her pleas for help. Jesus explained his cold response to the gentile woman by saying that he was sent only to help "the lost sheep of the house of Israel." *Matthew 15:24*. The woman continued to plead for help from Jesus, to which he responded, "It is not meet to take the children's bread, and cast it to the dogs." *Matthew 15:26*. The woman responded to this by saying, "Truth, Lord: yet the dogs eat of the crumbs which fall from their masters' table." *Matthew 15:27*. Jesus responded to what the woman said by saying, "O, woman, great is thy faith: be it unto thee even as thou wilt." *Matthew 15:28*. Jesus then healed her daughter.

Many might find it offensive that Jesus showed a reluctance to help this woman because she was not Jewish. Then, Jesus compared her status to that of a dog. Jesus healed her daughter because he was impressed by how she was willing to demean herself by acknowledging her status as a dog begging for crumbs from the table. Comparing any woman to a dog today would get most men "cancelled" immediately. But, even for back then, what Jesus said might seem impolite to say the least. She was in distress and pleading for help.

Shortly before the betrayal of Jesus by Judas, there was an incident in Bethany in which a woman anointed Jesus king of Israel with very expensive ointment. Matthew and Mark place this event at the house of one Simon the leper. *Matthew 26:6; Mark 14:3*. Luke places the event at the home of an unnamed Pharisee. *Luke 7:36*. John places the incident at the home of Mary, Martha, and Lazarus—the Lazarus whom Jesus had raised from the dead. *John 12:1-2*.

In Matthew and Mark, the woman is unidentified. *Matthew 26:7; Mark 14:3*. In Luke, the woman is identified only as "a woman in the city, which was a sinner." *Luke 7:37*. In John, however, the woman is clearly identified as Mary of Bethany, a woman who was close to Jesus and from a family to whom Jesus was very close as well. *John 12:3*.

All four of the Gospels agree that this incident took place at a home in Bethany. Otherwise, there is disagreement as to whose home it was and the identity of the woman who anointed Jesus with the ointment. It is possible that the Gospels describe separate yet similar incidents.

Luke tells us that the sinful woman from the city "stood at [Jesus's] feet behind him weeping, and began to wash his feet with tears, and did wipe them with the hairs of her head, and kissed his feet, and anointed them with the ointment." *Luke 7:38*. Jesus permitted—and even encouraged—the woman to wash and kiss his feet right there in front of his host and all of the guests in the house. When Jesus sensed that everyone was annoyed and possibly disgusted at this display, he told a parable, the point of which was to show that the woman was showing gratitude to Jesus for his mercy and forgiveness. The woman continued to kiss his feet even as Jesus was sitting there conversing with everyone. Jesus then chastises everyone in the room by saying, "Thou gavest me no kiss: but this woman since the time I came in hath not ceased to kiss my feet." *Luke 7:45*. There was a subtle implication that they should all have been kissing his feet. This, no doubt, rubbed the people in the room the wrong way. Jesus then says to the woman, "Thy sins are forgiven. ... Thy faith has saved thee; go in peace. *Luke 7:48-50*. Once again, a woman seemingly gets a response from Jesus by demeaning herself in his presence.[11] The people at this gathering were put off by this whole incident, thinking that Jesus was perhaps becoming too full of himself. Luke tells us that they "began to say within themselves, Who is this that forgiveth sins also? *Luke 7:49*. For whatever reason, Jesus did not seem to convey a sense of humility while among these people.

Matthew and Mark place this incident just prior to the betrayal of Jesus by Judas Iscariot. In John's Gospel it is Judas who objects to the woman's use of expensive ointment for her anointing of Jesus most vociferously by saying, "Why was not this ointment sold for three hundred pence, and given to the poor?" *John 12:5*. Jesus responded to Judas by saying, "Let her alone: against the day of my burying hath she kept this. For the poor always ye have with you; but me ye have not always." *John 12:7-8*. Judas may very well have betrayed Jesus because he felt that Jesus was getting a little too big for his britches, so to speak. Judas watched as in three short years, he saw that Jesus went from being a humble rural preacher to a man who was very comfortable being anointed king of Israel by a woman who was kissing his feet and washing them with her hair.

Scripture tells us that, on the very next day after that gathering at Bethany, Jesus rode into Jerusalem on a donkey while being hailed by the people as the new king of Israel. *John 12:12-19*. The people "[t]ook branches of palm trees, and went forth to meet him, and cried,

Hosanna: Blessed is the King of Israel that cometh in the name of the Lord." *John 12:13*. Any thoughts that Judas, or anyone else, may have had about Jesus becoming too big for his britches was surely cemented by Jesus's entry into Jerusalem.

His disciples did not understand what was happening when Jesus rode into Jerusalem on the donkey. *John 12:16*. Accepting all of this praise from people, first the anointing with ointment from the woman who kissed and washed his feet with her hair, and now this, a large crowd hailing him as their royal king. Where was the humble country-dweller? The one who once told his disciples that

> the princes of the Gentiles exercise dominion over them, and they that are great exercise authority upon them. But it shall not be so among you: but whoever will be great among you, let him be your minister; And whosoever will be chief among you, let him be your servant: Even as the Son of man came not to be ministered unto, but to minister.

Matthew 20:25-28. It is clear that Judas, and perhaps inwardly some of Jesus's other disciples, began to suspect that Jesus was beginning to succumb to the temptation of earthly power and glory that he tried so hard to resist. Three years prior, Satan had tempted Jesus with such earthly power and glory, but he resisted. *Luke 4:5-8*. Perhaps now, some may have thought, the lure of earthly power was beginning to be too much, even for Jesus.

Jesus's closest disciples did not view him as perfect. They questioned some of the things he said and did. They put their faith and trust in him, but they were also constantly vigilant. They would ask Jesus questions privately about his parables because they didn't understand what he was getting at. *Mark 4:10; 7:17; Luke 8:9*. His disciples asked Jesus why they were unable to cast out a demon. *Matthew 17:19*. To his disciples, Jesus was a great teacher, and perhaps a great prophet. But ultimately he was a man just like them.

Jesus's disciples did not view him as the theological enigma that he would later become for the church. They didn't ponder his nature and his divinity and such. Jesus was not yet seen as the Incarnation of God.

In his day, Jesus was seen as a prophet. *Matthew 21:11,46; Luke 7:39, 24:19; John 4:19,44, 6:14, 7:40,52; Acts 7:37.* Jesus referred to himself as a prophet. *Matthew 11:9, 13:57; Mark 6:4; Luke 4:24, 7:26.* A prophet need not be perfect or flawless. A prophet is a flawed human being who is called to speak for God. That's the way Jesus was perceived. That's the way Jesus saw himself. Scripture tells us that Jesus's disciples did not begin to put together most of what the church teaches about the fulness of Christ until *after* the Crucifixion. *John 12:16.*

Any imperfections or flaws that Jesus may have had—because he was human—would not negate his calling as a prophet from God.

***

Jesus took the impression of God that most had inherited from their forefathers, and took it to a whole new level. He supplanted the Abrahamic/Mosaic God with his Sermon on the Mount God.

I would say that if you're only going to commit to read three chapters in the entire Bible, those three chapters should be the Sermon on the Mount—chapters 5, 6, and 7 of the Gospel according to Matthew. The whole Sermon is only about three, maybe four, pages long in any copy of the Bible. It can be read online for free by those who don't own a Bible.

The contrast between the Abrahamic/Mosaic God and the God of Jesus is what is referenced in the New Testament where it says, "For the law was given by Moses, but grace and truth came by Jesus Christ." *John 1:17.*

Reading the Sermon on the Mount is what drew me to Jesus more than anything else. In my opinion, the heart of Jesus is clearly conveyed in these three biblical chapters. In the Sermon, I found a Jesus who taught that

- God has a special place in his heart for people who are kind and merciful even when they may be going through suffering caused by the unkindness and lack of mercy of others. *Matthew 5:1-12.* And taught that such people are "the salt of the earth" and "the light of the world." *Matthew 5:13-16.*

- men—in the very patriarchal society of his day—should respect women. *Matthew 5:27-32.*

- it's fine to love people who love us in return—but that's no major accomplishment. The challenge is to love people who *don't* love us back—even those who hate us. *Matthew 5:38-48*.

- we have a God who is "Our Father which art in heaven." *Matthew 6:9*.

Jesus's Sermon on the Mount God is radically different from the Abrahamic/Mosaic in many meaningful ways. The Sermon on the Mount God

- does not kill people in fits of anger or grief, *Genesis 7:10*, but rather he "maketh his sun to rise on the evil and on the good," *Matthew 5:45*.

- wouldn't lead his people into war after war,[12] but instead says "Blessed are the peacemakers." *Matthew 5:9*.

- would never make a woman accused of adultery undergo the bitter water test,[13] but shifts at least some of the responsibility for adultery on men by saying that "whosoever looketh on a woman to lust after her hath committed adultery with her already in his heart." *Matthew 5:28*.

- says—in response to the Abrahamic/Mosaic God saying, "Breach for breach, eye for eye, tooth for tooth," *Leviticus 24:20*—"But I say unto you, That ye resist not evil: but whosoever shall smite thee on thy right cheek, turn to him the other also." *Matthew 5:39*.

Jesus raised the standard. He challenges us to "Be ye therefore perfect, even as your Father which is in heaven is perfect." *Matthew 5:48*. He encourages us to adopt an impression of a perfect God who would never do an imperfect thing.

At the conclusion of the Sermon, it says that "when Jesus had ended these sayings, the people were astonished at his doctrine: For he taught them as one having authority, and not as the scribes." *Matthew 7:28-29*. Scribes had three major roles in the days of Jesus. They transcribed copies of the Scriptures, they studied and interpreted Scripture, and they taught from Scripture.[14] When the scribes taught people, they simply told them what the Scriptures say, and gave them some interpretation of it. Jesus's audience, during the Sermon on the Mount, was astonished at his teaching because he wasn't teaching out of any book. Jesus was giving them his *own* impressions of God.

ORIGINAL TRAUMA

In the earliest days of the Church, God went from being the God of Abraham, Isaac, and Jacob to being the God of Jesus Christ. *Ephesians 1:17*. The collective impression of God, for Christians, shifted from the Abrahamic/Mosaic God to the God of Jesus Christ.

Jesus taught us how to pray to his Sermon on the Mount God. It is the will of God that we should not try to be so conspicuous about it, so that everyone sees us as so prayerful and pious. Jesus said that hypocrites do that. *Matthew 6:5*. He said that when we pray, we should pray in secret. We should go into a room, shut the door, and pray to our Father alone. *Matthew 6:6*. This can be a powerful demonstration of one's hope or belief in the existence of God.

We should pray not just for ourselves but for our neighbors, and others in our lives as well. We should refer to God not just as "*my* Father" but as "*our* Father." *Matthew 6:9*. We should pray for *our* daily bread, forgiveness for *our* sins, and that God deliver *us* from evil—not just give me *my* daily bread, and forgive *my* sins, and deliver *me* from evil. *Matthew 6:11-13*.

Jesus taught that when we pray, we don't need to say the same things over and over again. He referred to this as "vain repetitions." *Matthew 6:7*. We can speak to our Father from our hearts—and we don't need to constantly beg God to love us and give us what we need, "for your Father knoweth what things ye have need of, before ye ask him." *Matthew 6:8*.

Jesus taught us

- that our true treasure is our treasure in heaven. *Matthew 6:19-24*.
- not to worry so much. *Matthew 6:25-34*.
- not to be judgmental toward others. *Matthew 7:1-5*.
- to beware of false prophets. *Matthew 7:15-20*.
- not to be just hearers of his teachings but doers of them. *Matthew 7:21-27*.

All of these things from the Sermon on the Mount strike me as integrous and sincere—things that God would actually say. When I say that I believe in Jesus, I mean that I believe in the Sermon on the Mount God as presented by Jesus. This is not to say that I don't believe that the rest of Scripture has value. On the contrary, I believe all of Scripture is priceless. But I do believe that the impression of God that works best for me, is the impression of God presented by Jesus Christ—specifically, the impression of God presented by Jesus in the Sermon on the Mount.

In this regard, I agree with Mahatma Gandhi (1869-1948), who famously read the entire Bible, and then honed in on the Sermon on the Mount as something with which he was wholeheartedly in agreement.[15] The wisdom of the Sermon is self-evident. It does not require contortions of one's conscience in order to accept. The Sermon presents an ethic which can be adopted and relied upon regardless of one's religious tradition. I believe we would all do well to live by the Sermon on the Mount.

***

Jesus spent about three years, in his public ministry, telling everyone who would listen about his Father in heaven. He told people that his Father was perfect. *Matthew 5:48.* He likened his Father to a shepherd who would leave his ninety-nine sheep to look for his one lost sheep. *Matthew 18:12-14.* Jesus spoke of a loving Father who would never give his children a stone if they asked for bread, or a snake if they asked for a fish. *Matthew 7:11-12.* His Father would never be so inconsiderate toward his children.

Jesus taught that people felt abandoned, betrayed, and rejected by God because they had a wrong impression of God. *Luke 4:18-19.* Jesus encouraged everyone to believe in the God who Moses said would never leave them nor forsake them. *Deuteronomy 31:8.* But after years of being his Father's number one cheerleader—telling everyone how kind, merciful, and perfect his Father is—Jesus found himself in a situation in which he too would feel abandoned, betrayed, and rejected by his God. According to the Gospels of Matthew and Mark—after suffering greatly at the hands of the ancient Romans, and then being nailed to the Cross—at about 3PM on that fateful Friday, Jesus cried out with a loud voice, "My God, my God, why hast thou forsaken me?" *Matthew 27:46; Mark 15:34.* He too felt the abandonment and betrayal from God that was experienced by so many others before him, and so many after him as well.

Was his mission a failure? The answer to this question depends first upon whether one believes in the Resurrection of Jesus. It further

141

depends on what is meant by Resurrection. Jesus described Resurrection as follows: "Verily, verily, I say unto you, Except a corn of wheat fall into the ground and die, it abideth alone: but if it die, it bringeth forth much fruit." *John 12:24*. In this light, the way of understanding the Resurrection is that Jesus died, and now he lives on within us all. *Galatians 2:20*. This is the operative way that the Resurrection changes lives. This makes Jesus's mission an epic success because, in dying as a corn of wheat, his death gave rise to a global wheat field of which you and I can be a part. In fact, one of Jesus's parables compares the kingdom of God to a field of wheat. *Matthew 13:24-30*. If this vision of the Resurrection of Jesus works for you, adopt it. After all, it comes from Jesus himself.

Scripture says that Jesus rose from the dead. *Matthew 28:16-20; Mark 16:14-20; Luke 24:36-53; John 20-21*. But Scripture also says that we all can be resurrected from the dead—just like Jesus. *1 Corinthians 15:12-58; 1 John 3:2*. The whole purpose of revealing the Resurrection of Christ is to give us hope that we too can look forward to being resurrected as well. *John 11:25-26*.

The nature of Jesus's resurrected glorified body is unclear from Scripture. On the one hand, Jesus showed the apostles the wounds on his hands and feet from the Crucifixion, and ate a meal to prove that he had been physically raised from the dead, and was not just a ghost. *Luke 24:36-43; John 20:20*. (This proof was apparently based on the belief that ghosts are incapable of eating.) On the other hand, the Risen Jesus was able to miraculously appear to people, sometimes in a form that was not immediately recognizable to them. *Luke 24:15-16,36; John 20:14,19*. Whatever the Resurrection appearances in the Gospels are supposed to mean, it is clear that what Jesus experienced was not portrayed as merely a resuscitation. Jesus's body had become a glorified body, the nature of which is left to pure speculation and belief.

Regarding the Resurrection of Jesus for people who are not Christian, it may suffice to believe that Jesus is still alive in the sense that everyone that God ever created is still alive. Jesus once had a discussion with some Jewish leaders "which say there is no resurrection." *Mark 12:18*. Jesus reminded them that when God first met Moses, God referred to himself as "the God of Abraham, and the God of Isaac, and the God of Jacob." *Mark 12:26*. The inference being that Abraham, Isaac, and Jacob—and everyone else we believe to be dead—are still alive. Jesus then said, "He is not the God of the dead, but the God of the living: ye therefore do greatly err." *Mark 12:27*. In response to our fear of death, *Hebrews 2:15*, Jesus essentially tells us there is no such thing as death—it's an illusion.

During the miracle of the Transfiguration, Jesus once appeared to the apostles Peter, James, and John in a transfigured form along with Moses and Elijah. *Matthew 17:1-8; Mark 9:2-8; Luke 9:28-36*. This was before the Crucifixion. Here, Jesus provides these three men of his inner circle with evidence that death is an illusion. He shows them that Moses and Elijah are still alive. Interestingly, in both cases, the Scripture is a bit murky about the deaths of those two men. In the case of Moses, the Scripture says that God himself buried Moses in the land of Moab, "but no man knoweth of his sepulchre unto this day." *Deuteronomy 34:6*. No human being ever knew where Moses was buried. Interesting. In the case of Elijah, Scripture does not say that he died at all. According to Scripture, Elijah was taken up into heaven by "a chariot of fire," never to be seen or heard from again. *2 Kings 2:11*. Jesus gave Peter, James, and John a glimpse—a vision showing that both Moses and Elijah were both alive and well in a way that the three apostles did not understand. *Luke 9:33*.

There is an interesting mention in the New Testament about a dispute between Michael the archangel and the devil, over the body of Moses. *Jude 1:9*. This is an apparent citation to an unknown written source which no longer exists. The devil was making the case that Moses did not deserve to rise from the dead to be with God because of his sinfulness. To which Michael the archangel replied to the devil, "The Lord rebuke thee."

***

According to his biblical genealogy, Jesus was a direct descendant of many of the people discussed here who inherited and passed along their childhood trauma to their own children. *Luke 3:31-38*. Did Jesus suffer from any generational trauma? Did Jesus experience childhood trauma? Did Jesus experience feelings of abandonment and rejection from God?

As may have been the case with David, while Jesus was growing up, his paternity was in question. Any childhood trauma that Jesus may have experienced probably stemmed largely from this. It is unlikely that many people in Nazareth, where Jesus was raised, believed in or even knew about the claim that he was the child of a virgin mother via a supernatural miracle. Even Joseph, knowing that he was not the father of the child Mary was carrying, wanted to part ways with her after he was told she was pregnant. He initially believed that she must have had committed sexual sin. *Matthew 1:19.*

Jesus probably had to deal with people whispering and passing along rumors about how his mother got pregnant out of wedlock. A very scandalous circumstance back then. On one occasion in Scripture, Jesus's enemies used his questionable paternity during an argument when they made an *ad hominem* attack, and said to him, "We be not born of fornication." *John 8:41.*

Jesus's empathetic and forgiving attitude towards women accused of sexual sin, *John 8:7,* may have stemmed from the trauma of his own mother going through life with a scarlet letter cloud hanging over her head.

The emphasis I placed on Jesus being human—along with all of the imperfections that must go with that—was meant largely to make the case that Jesus must have been subject to inherited generational trauma just like the rest of us. Generational trauma is part of the human condition in which we all share. If the intent of the Incarnation was to have God experience the human condition, then Jesus's humanity must have been full and genuine—trauma and all. *Hebrews 4:14-15.*

***

While in the Garden of Gethsemane with his disciples, Jesus was faced with the reality that he was about to be crucified. He decided to go off alone to pray. He told his disciples, "My soul is exceeding sorrowful, even unto death." *Matthew 26:38.* While praying, Jesus got so stressed out that

> there appeared an angel unto him from heaven, strengthening him. And being in an agony he prayed more earnestly: and his sweat was as it were great drops of blood falling down to the ground.

Luke 22:43-44. This was clearly a traumatic experience for Jesus. His sense of abandonment and rejection from God was beginning to build.

In Jesus's most trying time, he vehemently prayed to his Father, in the Garden of Gethsemane, to possibly spare him from what was to come. Did he feel like he got a stone or a snake from his Father then?

It was Jesus's destiny to experience the full extent of the trauma that goes with feeling abandoned, rejected, and betrayed by God. Perhaps, this is what was meant when John the Baptist described Jesus as "the Lamb of God, which taketh away the sin of the world." *John 1:29.*

***

I was a child much like any other, who grew in age and wisdom,[16] with the help of my parents, who were there for me until I became a full-grown man.[17] I grew up with my parents in Nazareth. They raised me well.

My father, Joseph, was a carpenter, a trade which he would eventually teach me.[18] My mother and father were good people. They were full of faith in God.

The news of my mother's pregnancy caused a problem in my parents' relationship initially.[19] I was born into a precarious situation. My mother was found to be pregnant before she married my father. In a world that doesn't believe in miracles, this was a problem for us—the fallout of which would span my entire life on this earth. As far back as I can remember, there were whispers about my mother, there were rumors about her.[20] This bothered me greatly, because I knew my mother was a righteous woman who loved God. She did not deserve to have such rumors spread about her like that. As a family, we made a concerted effort over time to smooth over the rumors and whispers.

The circumstances into which I was born would follow me into my adult life. Some people were so rude as to throw my suspected illegitimate status in my face.[21] After I started preaching and teaching publicly, some people wanted to discredit anything that I had to say about God, because my birth was supposedly illegitimate. The persistent rumors about my mother, which I remember hearing even as a child, are probably the reason I would always find it annoying when any woman was accused of sexual sin, whether true or not. On those occasions when a woman was accused of adultery or fornication in my presence, I would intercede on her behalf.[22] I did that because I thought of my mother, and the rumors which—if turned into formal accusations—could very well have resulted in her being stoned to death for fornication.[23]

As I was growing up, I had a burgeoning abiding sense that the purpose of my life was to do the will of God—who I learned to know as my Father in heaven.[24] ...Joseph was a good man. He was a good father. He raised me right. But he was not my <u>Father</u>. My Father was God in heaven.

When I was about twelve years old, I had an encounter with my heavenly Father in the Temple in Jerusalem while on a visit there with my family on our annual trip to Jerusalem for Passover.[25] That encounter was so intense that I did not head back to Nazareth with my parents when they left for home. After starting their journey home, they realized I was not with them, after traveling for a whole day. They had to turn around to come and get me. It took them three days to find me.[26] When they finally found me, my mother took me to task for making them so worried and anxious. I responded to them in a way that maybe they thought was a bit snide. I asked them, "Why are you even looking for me? Didn't you know that I have to be about my Father's business?"[27] I don't think they understood or appreciated that response.

After my father Joseph passed away, I spent a good part of my life working hard and looking after my mother.[28]

My cousin John was called by God to be a prophet in Israel.[29] He had a large following. He was very courageous in that he spoke truth to very powerful people.[30] He didn't seem to care that, often enough, his prophetic words were not well received by them. John believed that I too was sent by God. He told people that my time had come and that I was going to be a greater prophet than him.[31] One day, I went to be baptized by him in the Jordan River.[32] I began to publicly do my Father's business, which I began to learn about in the Temple when I was twelve. Unfortunately, my cousin John was killed not too long after I was baptized by him.[33]

God—my Father in heaven—is perfect.[34] But that doesn't mean that my relationship with him was without some difficulty. I don't mean that we had any negative issue between the two of us at all. What I mean is that my purpose in life was to do his perfect will in this world, and that was not easy.

My Father put me to the test more than once.

Shortly after my baptism, my Father sent me out into the desert to be tempted by Satan. Satan was not there to mess around. Satan tempted me with bread after I had fasted for forty days and nights, in a hot and arid desert.[35] He tempted me with all kinds of wealth and power.[36] He tempted me with everything a man could ever want. He held nothing back.

146

Everything at his disposal was made available to me for the asking. And he indeed had the power to give me all of that. ...It was tempting indeed.[37] But I resisted the temptation by constantly reminding myself of my Father's will. I kept reciting all of the relevant Scripture passages that came to mind. In fact, I rejected all of Satan's temptations every time by quoting Scripture passages to him—and myself.

Satan, who is very powerful, pulled out all the stops in his effort to get me to worship him. He tried to take advantage of the weakened state I was in because I had fasted for so long. At times I did ask myself why my Father was allowing all of this to happen,[38] allowing Satan to tempt me so much and so hard. I started to feel abandoned by my Father during that experience. But I was determined to follow my Father's will instead of mine, whatever the outcome.[39]

Worshipping Satan was simply not an option.

I never had an experience as intense, as frightening, and as filled with anxiety again.[40] Never, that is, until I had to face and experience crucifixion.

For about three years, I told everyone who would listen about the Lord God, my Father in heaven. I told everyone that my Father loved them, and that he wanted to be their Father too. I called my Father, "our Father" because I believed him to be the true Father of us all. And I wanted everyone to see him as their Father too. So, when the time came, it was difficult to accept that my Father—whose unconditional love I had extolled to everyone for years—was about to subject me to a level of suffering which made my temptation by Satan in the desert pale by comparison.

Yes, at times I asked myself, "Why?"[41] ...But, my Father's will be done.

It became clear that my temptation experience in the desert was meant to prepare me for what was about to happen.

When I knew that my arrest and execution were imminent, I prayed to my Father in a garden in Gethsemane.[42] I was scared. I was stressed out. I experienced indescribable anxiety. I did not want to be tortured and killed. Who would? Desiring something like that would be insane. I begged my Father repeatedly to spare me from that fate. Perhaps, I pleaded, there was another less torturous way for me to do his will, which I so desired to accomplish. I was so stressed, that blood started to drip out of my pores.[43] I was in agony. So much so that my Father sent an angel from heaven to strengthen me.[44]

My Father did not answer my prayer. Or, rather, his silence meant that his answer was no. No change in plan. I was to face the torture which awaited me. My Father did send the angel. But, at that point, I began to experience that uneasy feeling that my Father was going to make me feel completely abandoned again—a worse abandonment than I felt while getting tempted by Satan in the desert a few years prior.[45] Still, I kept hoping against hope that my Father would answer my prayer even at the eleventh hour. Perhaps, he was waiting to perform a dramatic rescue at the last second in front of everybody, thereby vindicating me before them all. ...That rescue didn't happen. It became clear that the end of my suffering would only be accomplished by my death.[46]

My feelings of abandonment continued to build as the subsequent events unfolded.[47] I was arrested. I was interrogated. I was put on trial twice and convicted both times. I was tortured and mocked by some Roman soldiers.[48] And finally, I would be nailed to the cross.

I felt completely abandoned and betrayed by my God—my Father.[49] I began to more deeply understand why there are people who have no trust or faith in my Father whatsoever. I began to more deeply understand what many people go through when they cry out to God with all of their hearts, in their most dire circumstances, only to be met with deafening silence which makes them feel abandoned, alone, and rejected by him. I began to more deeply understand why many people, in response to experiencing this feeling of abandonment by God—or observing how others feel such abandonment—choose not to believe that my Father even exists.[50]

My Father left me there to suffer extreme humiliation and pain. I could hear some of the people mocking me while I was on the cross, saying things to me like, "Come on Jesus, you saved others, let's see you save yourself now."[51]

...I forgave them all,[52] because that's what my Father would want me to do. Even then, as abandoned as I felt by him, I was determined to do his will.

I asked my Father to forgive them because they didn't really know what they were doing.[53] They mocked me and hated me, and thought I was against God. But that's because they were going by their own false impressions of God. They didn't know my Father. They didn't know him as I did. I tried to reconcile them with my Father—our Father. They didn't seem to want to know him.

But did I really know him? ...I was beginning to wonder.

I could feel the crowd's pain, their brokenheartedness, their sorrow, their anger, their feelings of abandonment, betrayal, and rejection from God. I could feel it. I could feel it all.

I wanted to take away their pain. I wanted to take away all of the trauma that was keeping them from seeing and knowing my Father as I did.[54] I wanted to take away all of the things that stood between them and their Father—my Father.

But I began to feel as if I no longer knew him. As if I no longer knew my Father. I thought, "Where was he? Why was he allowing all of this to happen to me?"

My own feeling of abandonment by my Father became very strong. I had kept my feelings of abandonment to myself, and had not expressed that to my Father in prayer until this point. In trying moments, I had made a habit of quoting Scripture in support of maintaining full faith in my Father no matter what, as I had done while being tempted in the desert. I did this, and I taught others to do the same.

I had lost all hope that my Father would rescue me.

Oh, the pain of all those people. I felt all of it. ...All of it.

I felt weak.

I felt thirsty.[55]

The weight of all of their pain. I began to feel the same pain and fear as those people who hated me. Of those who mocked me.

Was I being given their pain for me to feel?

Abandonment, loneliness, alienation, fear.

It was overwhelming. So overwhelming!

In my final state of exasperation, I quoted Scripture. This time not to express my faith and confidence in my Father, but rather to tell him how I felt. At this point, I felt so abandoned, so betrayed, so alone, so unloved, that I couldn't even call him "Father."[56]

I quoted a psalm of David, and yelled to my Father, in as loud a voice as I could muster in my weakened state, "MY GOD! MY GOD! WHY HAVE YOU FORSAKEN ME?!"[57]

***

The moment when Jesus asked God why he had forsaken him, and then died, is depicted on every Crucifix. Too many of us pass by crucifixes all the time without giving what it depicts a second thought.

149

Whenever I see a crucifix anywhere, I try to take at least a moment to recall the fact that it depicts the moment that Jesus died feeling betrayed and stabbed in the back by the Father he taught others to trust. That's a deep paradox to ponder.

There are people suffering every day in this world. Many of them go through unimaginable suffering. Many of them reach out to God and do not seem to get relief. Then they ask, as Jesus did on the Cross, "Why, God?" When Jesus experienced abandonment and betrayal from God, he connected with all of those people—with all of us.

This aspect of the Crucifixion is glossed over by too many Christians. Catholics, for example, recite our Profession of Faith every Sunday during Mass. Regarding the Crucifixion, we say, "For our sake he was crucified under Pontius Pilate, he suffered death and was buried." The words "he suffered death" don't begin to touch upon what Jesus experienced on the Cross. The real suffering—perhaps *the* most significant aspect of the Crucifixion—is that while he was dying, Jesus experienced what it feels like to believe one has been abandoned by God. That feeling of abandonment, betrayal, and rejection from God *is* the inherited generational trauma depicted in the Bible. The one thing that all of the biblical generations experienced—from Adam & Eve all the way down to Jesus—is that sense of abandonment, betrayal, and rejection from God.

***

What was it about Jesus that so motivated the powers that be of his day to want him dead? What did he teach that so upset them? What was it that set them off? If you think about it, Jesus's teachings were not anything so earth-shaking or new. He taught people to love each other, hardly something deserving capital punishment. He didn't really teach anything that wasn't somewhere in Scripture already. So, what was it? What did he say or do that triggered so many powerful people to conspire against him?

Jesus taught people to rely on their *own* impressions of God, rather than the impressions of God taught to them by the powers that be and their ancestors. In doing so, Jesus made the religious leaders of his day feel like he was negating and nullifying their purpose as conduits and mediators between the people and their God.

Jesus taught that we have a Father in heaven, and that we can trust our *own* impressions of that Father. Our previous false impressions of God were what was standing in the way of a meaningful relationship with our Father. We may have gotten these false impressions from the very people charged with teaching us about God. But by forming our own impressions of God with the help of Jesus, and our own Genesis 18 Abraham, we can know a more intimate, loving, forgiving, and approachable God. We can then indeed know God, despite his inscrutability on a cognitive level. This is why, as a result of Jesus's teachings, Scripture tells us, "Let us therefore come boldly unto the throne of grace, that we may obtain mercy, and find grace in time of need." *Hebrews 4:16*. We can approach God ourselves, without the mechanisms of organized religion. This, of course, infuriated the leaders of organized religion, who depended on religion for their livelihood. *John 8:40*.

Jesus was crucified specifically because he encouraged people to escape the unbroken cycle of inherited generational trauma by forming their *own* impression of God for themselves. He invited people to *think*. His parables invited people to draw their *own* conclusions.

After the religious leaders of Jesus's day successfully got the Romans to execute Jesus, the message of Jesus began to spread. The Church began to add thousands of members very quickly. *Acts 2:41*. Gentiles began rejecting their Greek and Roman gods in favor of the gospel of Jesus. Some Jews as well began supplanting the impression of God that they grew up with, in favor of the gospel of Jesus. This was people of many backgrounds using their newly discovered freedom to worship the impression of God of their choosing, according to their own consciences. *Acts 2:9-10*. All of these people were risking persecution for doing this. It was an exercise in religious liberty some 1,800 years before the First Amendment of the United States Constitution. It must have been inspiring for those who were there to witness it.

It did not take long, however, for religious leaders to fight back. Church leaders throughout history, who claimed to be exclusive representatives of Jesus, negated the freedom to go by one's own impressions of God that Jesus tried to teach people. They suppressed this aspect of Jesus's teachings. So, this aspect of the gospel went full circle. It went from Jesus teaching people to use their own consciences to form their own impressions of God, to the Church forming its own authoritarian impressions of Jesus, and demanding that people go by the Church's impressions, not their own. This was sometimes enforced by the Church under threat of execution for heresy.

Jesus encouraged people to judge for themselves what is right. *Luke 12:57*. The religious leaders of Jesus's day did not like the way Jesus encouraged people to think for themselves and form their own impressions of God. They wanted their followers to adopt *their* impressions of God as unassailable truth. Unfortunately, my own Church—the Roman Catholic Church—has been guilty of this.

There are countless martyrs throughout history who were put to death—or otherwise punished—as heretics, for having a different impression of God than the Church leaders at the time. Many of these "heretics" weren't even harming anyone. They were simply executed for voicing their views about God. One of the most glaring examples of this was the case of St. Joan of Arc—a teenage girl who was burned at the stake for claiming that St. Catherine of Siena, and other saints, spoke to her, and for sharing her visions from God.[58] As a result, the Church's impression of God at the time told the bishops, "Just kill this b*tch!"

The justification for her execution came—at least in part—from the Scripture passage which says, "Thou shalt not suffer a witch to live." *Exodus 22:18*. This passage really means that if a woman starts to think for herself, and forms and voices her own impressions of God instead of blindly adopting the impressions of her religious leaders as instructed—kill her.

Every time we gaze upon a crucifix—in addition to causing us to reflect on Jesus's sense of abandonment from God as he took his last breaths—it should serve as a reminder that this is what can happen to people who encourage others to form their own impressions of God, i.e., to think for themselves. No less than fifteen times in the New Testament, Jesus is quoted as saying, "But I say unto you…"[59] Usually when he said this, it was after he had referred to a teaching that his listeners had derived from their understanding of something in the Old Testament. Jesus was asking his audience to substitute the impression of God they had formed from their understanding of the Abrahamic/Mosaic God, with the impression of God that Jesus offered them. Jesus respected, however, that each individual's impression of God was their own to form.

Jesus

***

The truth is that every human being—no matter who it is—can at most have and offer an *impression* of God. That's the most we're ever going to get from anybody. Problems occur when people believe that *their* impressions of God are objective truth, and that any alternate impressions of God must be inaccurate or—even worse—lies from the devil. No one has a direct line to God. Those that think they do are just deluded. Scripture is very clear that, "No man hath seen God at any time." *John 1:18.*

Organized religion all too often is based on forcing, coercing, or otherwise convincing people to adopt the religious leaders' impressions of God as objective, unbiased, and completely accurate truths about God. Organized religion will often discourage independent thinking about God.

All too often, organized religion gets people to adopt impressions of God that are wrong and destructive to their own sense of self. They don't feel loved by their God at all.

"God hates me."

"God hates me because I'm worthless and unworthy."

"God hates me because of my race."

"God hates me because of my gender."

"God hates me because I don't go to church."

"God hates me because I don't belong to the right faith community."

"God hates me because I'm not chaste."

"God hates me because I'm gay and therefore an abomination."

"God hates me because I use my mind to think about what I actually believe about God."

These are all responses to actual impressions of God that various religious leaders try to get people to believe. And then—refusing to own their beliefs, or take responsibility for what their own consciences tell them, ignoring their inner Genesis 18 Abraham altogether—these religious leaders absolve themselves for teaching the oppressive things they want people to believe about themselves, and say something like, "Hey, it's not me. It's right there in the Bible."

The Christian teaching that we each have the right to form and rely upon our *own* impressions of God is right there in the New Testament.

Referring to Jesus, a prophecy in the New Testament says that

> he is the mediator of a better covenant, which was established upon better promises. For if that first covenant had been faultless, then should no place have been sought for the second.

Hebrews 8:6-7. This prophecy has God go on to say that the new covenant is meant to specifically supplant the old covenant "that [he] made with their fathers in the day when [he] took them by the hand to lead them out of the land of Egypt." *Hebrews 8:9.* And quotes God as saying, "I will put my laws into their mind, and write them in their hearts: and I will be to them a God, and they shall be to me a people." *Hebrews 8:10.* This prophecy acknowledges the God given power of each and every individual to form their own impression of God when—in it—God says,

> And they shall not teach every man his neighbour, and every man his brother, saying, Know the Lord: for all shall know me, from the least to the greatest.

Hebrews 8:11.[60] See? The God of Jesus speaks directly to the minds and hearts of *everyone.* That includes you. That includes me. Jesus said that the Holy Spirit "shall teach you all things, and bring all things to your remembrance." *John 14:26.* The knowledge of God that you need is already within you. Often, when Jesus taught, he reminded people that God speaks directly to everyone when he said, "He that hath ears to hear, let him hear." *Matthew 11:5; 13:9,43; Mark 4:9,23; 7:16; Luke 8:8; 14:35.*

Contrast this with how the Abrahamic/Mosaic God punished Moses's sister, Miriam, with leprosy, *Numbers 12:10,* for once asking, "Hath the LORD indeed spoken only by Moses? hath he not spoken also by us?" *Numbers 12:2.* Miriam was punished for suggesting that God spoke to her mind and heart—which is odd in that Miriam is referred to in Scripture as a "prophetess." *Exodus 15:20.* Ask your inner Genesis 18 Abraham, would your God have ever stricken somebody with leprosy simply for asking whether God speaks to them too? ...Is that *your* God—a God who strikes people with diseases for thinking that they can have a relationship with God on par with anyone else?

***

A developed conscience does not need to be taught right from wrong. People already know how to be. You know right from wrong. We all do. At this point in your life, you don't need anyone to give you a moral list of dos and don'ts. We all *choose* whether to do the right thing every day. But, come on, we always know what the right thing to do is. Although sometimes, tough choices require that we think things through or get good advice.

Jesus boiled down the entire Christian ethic into a couple of simple maxims. First there is the Golden Rule: Do unto others as you would have them do unto you. *Matthew 7:12.* This golden rule presupposes that everyone already knows how they should treat others. Just treat others the way you want to be treated. It's so simple. What is there to disagree with in this Golden Rule? The righteousness of this ethic is self-evident.

Second is Jesus's two commandments. The first is, "Thou shalt love the Lord thy God with all thy heart, and with all thy soul, and with all thy mind." *Matthew 22:37.* And the second is, "Thou shalt love thy neighbor as thyself." *Matthew 22:39.*[61] Jesus said that the second commandment is "like unto" the first one. *Matthew 22:39.* This means that the two commandments go hand in hand. We can't do one without doing the other.

However, there's something very important about Jesus's second commandment. It presupposes that we love ourselves. How can we love our neighbors as ourselves if we don't love ourselves? This is where our generational trauma might interfere with our ability to follow Jesus's commandments. Jesus's commandments presume a healthy self-image and self-esteem.

Too many people do not love themselves. Many are self-loathing, suffer from low self-esteem, or just out-and-out hate themselves.

Self-love is not the same as narcissism. Narcissism is a neurosis. Self-love means that you "accept yourself fully, treat yourself with kindness and respect, and nurture your growth and wellbeing."[62] It is self-love that helps us to strive to be our best selves. We're supposed to love others. But we cannot give of what we don't have. We must also have love for ourselves.

If we need help learning to love ourselves, it may be wise to seek professional help. The inability to love oneself is a big hindrance to loving others. Years of generational trauma may have done a number on us that we will need help overcoming. That's okay. There is no shame in getting the help that we need.

***

Jesus taught that people should obey the *spirit* of the law rather than just the *letter* of the law. He said that "God is a Spirit: and they that worship him must worship him in spirit and in truth." *John 4:24*. For a proper view of the law of Moses, I turn to the Sermon on the Mount. On the one hand, Jesus said,

> Think not that I am come to destroy the law, or the prophets: I am not come to destroy, but to fulfil. For verily I say unto you, Till heaven and earth pass, one jot or one tittle shall in no wise pass from the law, till all be fulfilled.

Matthew 5:17-18. Jesus did not intend to abrogate the law of Moses. He intended for people to abide by the true intent of the law.

One Sabbath day, Jesus and his disciples were hungry. So, the disciples walked through a corn field to pick ears of corn for themselves and Jesus to eat. *Mark 2:23*. Some religious leaders witnessed this and asked Jesus, "Behold, why do they on the sabbath day that which is not lawful?" *Mark 2:24*. In his response, Jesus said, "The sabbath was made for man, and not man for the sabbath." *Mark 2:27*. Jesus's point being that the law of the Sabbath was meant to be a blessing. It was meant as a day of rest from the people's burdens. But the religious leaders who spoke to Jesus completely defeated the meaning of the Sabbath law by turning the law itself into a burden. They used the Sabbath as a rationale for forbidding hungry people from picking a few ears of corn for themselves because they had apparently interpreted that activity as "work" which the law forbids on the Sabbath.

The law of the Sabbath comes from the Ten Commandments.

> Remember the sabbath day, to keep it holy. Six days shalt thou labour, and do all thy work: But the seventh day is the sabbath of the LORD thy God: in it thou shalt not do any work, thou, nor thy son, nor thy daughter, thy manservant, nor thy maidservant, nor thy cattle, nor thy stranger that is within thy gates: For in six days the LORD made heaven and earth, the sea, and all that in them is, and rested the seventh day: wherefore the LORD blessed the sabbath day, and hallowed it.

Exodus 20:8-11. A plain reading of the Sabbath commandment shows that it was intended as a blessing. It commanded everyone to take a mandatory rest one day per week. And, if one had servants, or other employees, one had to give them *their* rest. One had to give one's children their rest too. Even cattle got their rest from this law.

This commandment would go on to be the foundational basis for workers' rights in the Western world. The five-day work week is based on the fact that Saturday is the Sabbath, and Sunday is the Lord's Day for Christians.

The men who confronted Jesus weaponized the Sabbath law, using it to try and force Jesus and his disciples to go hungry rather than pick a few ears of corn for themselves on that Sabbath day. They did not treat the law as a blessing. Jesus wanted them to focus on the *intent* of the law rather than a literal reading of it.

Regarding the intent of the law, Jesus said,

> Ye have heard that it was said by them of old time, Thou shalt not kill; and whosoever shall kill shall be in danger of the judgment: But I say unto you, That whosoever is angry with his brother without a cause shall be in danger of the judgment: and whosoever shall say to his brother, Raca [calling one worthless or foolish], shall be in danger of the council: but whosoever shall say, Thou fool, shall be in danger of hell fire.

Matthew 5:21-22. Jesus challenged his audience to do better. He said that people can avoid breaking the commandment against murder by

157

addressing the anger within that usually precedes a premeditated killing. By addressing the root cause of the sin before it happens, one can avoid the consequences of any punishment, and the harm that the sin causes, by dealing with it only after the sinful action has occurred.

With regard to having heard "an eye for an eye, and a tooth for a tooth," Jesus said, "But I say unto you, That ye resist not evil: but whosoever shall smite thee on thy right cheek, turn to him the other also." *Matthew 5:38-39; see also Luke 6:27.*

Jesus said the same thing about the commandment against committing adultery, "But I say unto you, That whosoever looketh on a woman to lust after her hath committed adultery with her already in his heart." *Matthew 5:28.* Again, Jesus addresses the root cause of the sin. He advises that people should check themselves while the sin is just a figment of their imaginations before it becomes a reality that may cause irreparable harm.

The gist of what Jesus taught regarding the law is that (1) the law should cause us to address the root causes of our sins (our trauma) *before* we commit serious wrongful actions, and (2) if we follow the "do unto others" Golden Rule faithfully, we'll be following the intent of the *whole* law without having to memorize all 613 provisions of the Mosaic law. *Matthew 7:12.*[63]

***

Jesus famously said, "I am the way, the truth, and the life: no man cometh unto the Father, but by me." *John 14:6.*[64] A bold statement, to be sure. In calling himself the way, the truth, and the life, I think Jesus meant that his teaching—that we should rely on our *own* impressions of God, according to our consciences—is the only way to God. He taught that if we wish to find God, we'll find God right there within us. He was there all along. This is the truth. This is the way. Finding God within ourselves is the only way to God. It is the only way to life.

In my humble estimation, I believe he was saying that false impressions of God are what keep people from God—the true God. Freeing ourselves from our false impressions of God is essential. This is the way to God.

Jesus offers his impression of God. But he also leaves it up to us to form our own impressions. He teaches that we already have consciences capable of recognizing rightful impressions of God. All we have to do—as did Genesis 18 Abraham—is use our own consciences to discern the truth about God. We should judge for ourselves what is right. *Luke 12:57.*

Many say that we must follow Jesus and "accept him as our Lord and Savior" in order to be saved and not go to hell. But, what does it mean to follow Jesus? What does it mean to "accept" him? In the Sermon on the Mount, Jesus explicitly says that following him is not just about praising his name and calling him, "Lord, Lord." *Matthew 7:21.* The Jesus bumper stickers, t-shirts, and other merch is not what it's about. Jesus said that we follow him by *doing* the will of our Father. And—this is for whoever needs to hear this—professing to believe in and follow Jesus is not the operative response. The operative response is to follow Jesus's commandments. And what are those commandments? Simply to abide by the "do unto others" Golden Rule. Anyone can do this. And those that do, are doing the will of our Father, regardless of whether they profess to be Christian or not.

> If ye love me, keep my commandments. ... If a man love me, he will keep my words: and my Father will love him, and we will come unto him, and make our abode with him. He that loveth me not keepeth not my sayings: and the word which ye hear is not mine, but the Father's which sent me.

John 14:15,23-24. It's doing the word, not just hearing it. *Matthew 7:26; 21:28-31; James 1:22.*

***

Many adults have maladaptive behaviors as the result of the trauma we may have experienced as children. Jesus did many healings during his years of public ministry, according to the Gospels. Those who believe that Jesus wants to heal our physical illnesses but not our mental illnesses are mistaken. When Jesus healed people who were said to be demon-possessed, he was healing their minds. Whether demons literally exist is for the reader to decide. The people Jesus dealt with were either actually demon-possessed, or believed themselves to be so.

Either way, the end result was the same—serious mental illness.

In one story, Jesus healed a man who spoke to Jesus as the demons within him saying, "My name is Legion: for we are many." *Mark 5:9.* Jesus cast the demons out of the man. The operative point, however, is that the man's mind was healed. The Scripture tells us that when the people came to see what had happened "they come to Jesus, and see him that was possessed with the devil, and had the legion, sitting, and clothed, and in his right mind." *Mark 5:15.* The man was "in his right mind," whereas before he was not. His mind was healed. And when Jesus healed people, he told them that *their faith* had made them whole. *Matthew 8:13, 9:22, 15:28; Mark 5:34; Luke 17:19, 18:42.* Jesus told them that God's healing power was within them all along. But they were convinced that they were powerless to know God or change their lives. So, they didn't. Jesus helped them to access their power within. Jesus addressed mental health more than he gets credit for. Jesus reached out to those who are weary with stress, anxiety, and depression when he said,

> Come unto me, all ye that labour and are heavy laden, and I will give you rest. Take my yoke upon you, and learn of me; for I am meek and lowly in heart: and ye shall find rest unto your souls. For my yoke is easy, and my burden is light.

Matthew 11:28-30.

***

I think many people have woefully underestimated the amount of trauma that has been spread due to false impressions of God. People often wonder why there have been so many atrocities committed in God's name throughout history. When, to explain this, one need only understand that the majority of the world's population—for thousands of years now—has believed in the Abrahamic/Mosaic God who himself is said to have wiped out everyone in a flood,[65] killed the firstborn sons of an entire nation,[66] inflicted plagues and diseases on people when he got angry at them,[67] encouraged his people to engage in war after war against people who worshipped other gods,[68] destroyed entire towns,[69] and actually suborned genocide.[70] Then people scratch

their heads and wonder why so many people—who were no doubt
traumatized by believing that the true God engaged in such behavior—
went on to commit acts similar to what the Abrahamic/Mosaic God is
said to have done himself, often in his name.

The number of people walking around feeling traumatized by God
is not negligible. This has caused some serious damage—from individuals having problems with relationships in their lives to global atrocities. You might think I'm overplaying the fallout from people having
harmful impressions of God. But the fruit from these harmful impressions is plain to see. Regarding those who knowingly teach others to
believe false impressions of God, and the damage they can do, Jesus
said in the Sermon on the Mount,

> Beware of false prophets, which come to you in sheep's
> clothing, but inwardly they are ravenous wolves. Ye
> shall know them by their fruits. Do men gather grapes
> of thorns, or figs or thistles? Even so every good tree
> bringeth forth good fruit; but a corrupt tree bringeth
> forth evil fruit. A good tree cannot bring forth evil
> fruit, neither can a corrupt tree bring forth good fruit.
> Every tree that bringeth not forth good fruit is hewn
> down, and cast into the fire. Wherefore by their fruits
> ye shall know them.

Matthew 7:15-20.

The Abrahamic/Mosaic God's reputation for causing all kinds of
havoc precedes him. Have you ever noticed that, when a natural disaster happens that ruins people's homes and lives, insurance companies
and others refer to it as "an act of God?"[71] That's because they're going
by the God they learned about from the time that they were children.
The vengeful God, who inflicts pestilence, plagues, and other disasters
on people, is part of their childhood trauma. The legal definition of
"act of God" is a natural disaster.[72] That should tell you something
right there. If people went more by Jesus's impression of God, "acts
of God" would be things like: someone unexpectedly being cured of a
horrible disease, peace happening when war was expected, oppressed
people getting justice, people falling in love, people rallying to the aid
of people in need—things like that.

I believe that Jesus tried to set things straight about God. He wanted to free people from their trauma inducing impressions of God. But the religious leaders of his day—who had a vested interest in controlling the impressions of God of others—would have none of it. They perceived Jesus's teachings as chipping away at their authority and power. They felt threatened. They felt that Jesus was interfering with their livelihoods and positions. Jesus had to go. So, in God's name, they sought the crucifixion of Jesus. Because, in their view, killing people who went around saying wrong things about God is what the Abrahamic/Mosaic God did and advocated in Scripture—so they followed that lead.

The teachings of Jesus were meant to liberate people and set them free. People needed to be free to believe what they wished about God—thereby being free to believe what they wished about themselves. Jesus said,

> If ye continue in my word, then are ye my disciples indeed; And ye shall know the truth, and the truth shall make you free. ... If the Son therefore shall make you free, ye shall be free indeed.

John 8:31-32,36. We can all live in this freedom. We can live in the covenant wherein "they shall not teach every man his neighbour, and every man his brother, saying, Know the Lord: for all shall know me, from the least to the greatest." *Hebrews 8:11.* We can all live in faith communities where each of us judges for ourselves what is right. *Luke 12:57.* We can live in a world where we can stand before any religious leaders and say "I have lived in all good conscience before God until this day" without being slapped in the face for saying so. *Acts 23:1.*

Jesus taught that some of the impressions of God of the religious leaders of his day—and even some of the impressions of God in Scripture—were wrong. These impressions of God actually served to traumatize people, even from the days of their childhood, making them fearful of the very God they were told to honor, worship, serve, and obey. Jesus sought to reintroduce everyone to the *true* God—the God he knew as his Father in heaven. This is how he sought to break the cycle of inherited generational trauma.

Jesus

***

Jesus offers us the way to break the cycle of inherited generational trauma and to rise above it. Knowing that the family is the source of most of the transmittal of the trauma, Jesus proposed a radical redefinition of family.

Jesus is often portrayed by many as being "pro-family." But quotes attributed to Jesus in Scripture suggest otherwise. When Jesus's mother and brothers were waiting outside of a synagogue to meet with him while he was speaking, someone told him that they were outside looking to see him. Jesus responded,

> Who is my mother? and who are my brethren? [pointing to his disciples] Behold my mother and brethren! For whosoever shall do the will of my Father which is in heaven, the same is my brother, and sister, and mother.

Matthew 12:48-50. Jesus's spiritual family took precedence over his natural family.

Regarding family—in a seldom quoted saying of Jesus—he said,

> Suppose ye that I am come to give peace on earth? I tell you, Nay; but rather division: For from henceforth there shall be five in one house divided, three against two, and two against three. The father shall be divided against the son, and the son against his father; the mother against the daughter, and the daughter against the mother; the mother in law against her daughter in law, and the daughter in law against her mother in law.

Luke 12:51-53. This is the opposite of what most Christians profess about Jesus regarding family, and peace on earth. Jesus, no doubt, had issues with the definition of family.

Family, which can be, and has been, a big blessing for many, is also the primary source of childhood trauma and the passing down of such trauma. So, to interrupt that pattern, what Jesus did is something that bears a striking resemblance to what modern psychology refers to as reparenting. Jesus encourages our "inner child" to replace our "inner

163

parent voice" with a new parent model—"Our Father which art in heaven." *Matthew 6:9.*

It was Carl Jung (1875-1961) who coined the term inner child.[73] The inner child is "the impressionable and vulnerable part of ourselves wounded and shaped throughout the earliest experiences and stages of our lives."[74] The adults that we eventually become are older, hopefully wiser, and hopefully more mature versions of our wounded inner child. Our inner child influences all of our decisions.

The decisions of our inner child are not necessarily rational. In fact, they often don't make sense at all when opened to scrutiny. Our inner child's decisions are based on all of the fears, angers, disappointments, emotions, hurts, and insecurities that we experienced as children. Our view of the world, which we developed as young children, stayed with us as we became adults. This explains our often childish responses to our adult problems.

These childish responses as adults can and do cause harm and pain. We do and say hurtful things. Our relationships suffer. In short, we engage in behavior that the Bible refers to as sin. Psychologists often say that the answer to dealing with mental illness is to heal our inner child. Children often have dysfunctional relationships with their parents, and their God. Scripture refers to healing our inner child, as reconciliation with God. *Romans 5:10.*

Many people who believe in God have a fear-filled relationship with God that includes a certain amount of distrust towards God. The teachings of Jesus involve a renewal and peace-making between ourselves and our prior impression of God. It requires us to admit that we had God all wrong. We blindly believed the impressions of others about God—and this caused us to have anger or hostility towards God, or to reject belief in God's very existence altogether. St. Paul of Tarsus spoke of his inner child when he wrote,

> When I was a child, I spake as a child, I understood as
> a child, I thought as a child: but when I became a man,
> I put away childish things.

1 Corinthians 13:11. Jesus implicitly said that his preaching was directed at our inner child when he said, "Verily I say unto you, Whosoever shall not receive the kingdom of God as a little child, he shall not enter therein." *Mark 10:15; Luke 18:17.*

When Jesus tells us that we have a Father in heaven who loves us, he is speaking to our inner child. If you think about it, a mature, mentally sound adult should have no need for new parent models any longer. But Jesus was aware of our need.

Scripture tells us very early on that Adam was created first and that Eve was created as a partner for him. God said, "It is not good that the man should be alone." *Genesis 2:18.* God goes on to say, "Therefore shall a man leave his father and his mother, and shall cleave unto his wife: and they shall be one flesh." *Genesis 2:24.* God's plan was that, as adults, most of us would leave our parents and go on to start families of our own. But, as we have seen, this plan has resulted in many family difficulties which the Bible documents. In many cases, because of the inherited generational trauma, families have become unmitigated disasters.

Without question, the single most significant thing that Jesus offers with regard to breaking the cycle of inherited generational trauma is very similar to what is referred to in psychology as reparenting.[75] The process of reparenting was introduced in the 1970s. It focused on getting adults to feel the feelings of value, love, and protection they may have lacked during childhood.[76] In reparenting therapy, the therapist assumes a parental role with the patient, thereby replacing or substituting a parent who may have been toxic to the patient, with a kind, loving, understanding parent in the person of the therapist. The crux of Jesus's message is that we have a Father in heaven who loves us and, unlike our earthly parents, is perfect, *Matthew 5:48.*

Hundreds of years before Jesus, Scripture said that God is "[a] father of the fatherless." *Psalm 68:5.* In its primary sense, this applied to orphans. Today, we would probably say, using inclusive language, that God is the parent of the parentless. In a larger sense, this can apply to those who may not have had loving, nurturing, supportive, and affirming parent figures in their lives. People without such parent figures can be said to be parentless, even if they did literally have parents.

Jesus reached out primarily to those in need of a loving, nurturing, supportive, and affirming parent in that larger sense. Jesus saw himself as a reconciler, reuniting lost children with their estranged parent, in the same way that the prodigal son was reunited with his father in one of Jesus's most famous parables. *Luke 15:10-32*.

Jesus, knew that *all* parents are flawed, as are all humans. All parents traumatize their children to one extent or another. We can't help it. But there can be within all of us, the voice of a perfect parent, upon which we can rely.

Recognizing our need for worthy parental figures, Jesus said, "And call no man your father upon the earth: for one is your Father, which is in heaven." *Matthew 23:9*. He didn't mean that we should neglect, disrespect, or abandon our parents. But he did mean that we all have a heavenly Father we can count on and have access to on our own, without needing the permission of any conduit or mediator. Jesus offered this relationship with our heavenly Father as the way to break the inherited generational trauma that has harmed us all. We have the freedom to have a relationship with our Father.

Sharing this simple message cost Jesus his life. The powers that be would not have it. Jesus died in vain if we cling to our old false impressions of God. Jesus asked for nothing less than the renewing of our minds. We need to let go and embrace the newness of his message.

Regarding the new message he preached, Jesus said,

> No man also seweth a piece of new cloth on an old garment: else the new piece that filled it up taketh away from the old, and the rent is made worse. And no man putteth new wine into old bottles: else the new wine doth burst the bottles, and the wine is spilled, and the bottles will be marred: but new wine must be put into new bottles.

Mark 2:21-22. It's our decision whether we wish to be new cloth and new bottles so that we can accept the new cloth and the new wine.

Jesus gave his life so that we could be in right relationship with our Father in heaven, and have a clearer understanding of who he is, by discarding the false impressions we may have had about him all along. This is the gospel message. Jesus died for us, that we might know God, the true God—the Sermon on the Mount God.

***

Lastly, this brings us to the one man who probably understood and appreciated Jesus's gospel of freedom more than any other human on the planet—St. Paul of Tarsus. What follows is my brief nod to St. Paul.

An Angel Comforting Jesus Before His Arrest in the Garden of Gethsemane
Carl Heinrich Bloch (1834-1890)

The Conversion of St. Paul
Caravaggio (1571-1610)

CHAPTER SIXTEEN

ST. PAUL OF TARSUS

"Yea, woe is unto me, if I preach not the gospel!"
-- 1 Corinthians 9:16

———

THE INFLUENCE OF St. Paul of Tarsus on the thought and theology of Christianity cannot be overstated. Some two-thirds of the New Testament content comes from writings attributed to him.[1] His contribution to the New Testament consists of some thirteen epistles to various churches throughout the ancient Mediterranean region which Paul founded or cofounded. Paul's impressions of God and Christ became the template for most of the Church's teachings.

Nothing is known about Paul's family, except that he is said to have had at least one sister and nephew. *Acts 23:16.* He identifies relatives named Andronicus, Junia, Herodion, Lucius, Jason, and Sosipater. *Romans 16:7,11,21.* And he made reference to a brother named Epaphroditus, *Philippians 2:25*, but he may have meant that Epaphroditus was his brother in the Lord.

Paul was—by his own account—Jewish. He claimed to be "of the tribe of Benjamin," and to have been a Pharisee. He was proud of his heritage, and boastfully described himself as a "Hebrew of the Hebrews." *Philippians 3:5.* (Whatever that's supposed to mean.)

His birth name was Saul, but he eventually went by the Greco-Roman version of his name—Paul.

Paul enters the biblical scene about three years after the crucifixion of Jesus. Scripture tells us that, at that time, "the word of God increased; and the number of the disciples multiplied in Jerusalem greatly; and a great company of the priests were obedient to the faith." *Acts 6:7.*

During that time there was a man named Stephen, who was "full of faith and power" and "did great wonders and miracles among the people." *Acts 6:8*. Stephen was a very popular preacher of the gospel of Jesus. Some Jewish religious leaders came against Stephen, disputing what he had to say, but according to Scripture, "they were not able to resist the wisdom and the spirit by which he spake." *Acts 6:9-10*.

The ire of the Jewish religious leaders against Stephen was not just because he taught that Jesus was the Messiah. The Jewish Sanhedrin dealt with messianic pretenders all the time. *Acts 5:34-40*. The specific reason(s) that the religious leaders targeted Stephen for investigation is that Stephen was spreading an impression of God, and the Scriptures, which with those Jewish leaders vehemently disagreed. Stephen's accusers said that they "heard him speak blasphemous words against Moses, and against God," *Acts 6:11*, and that

> [t]his man ceaseth not to speak blasphemous words against this holy place [the Temple], and the law; For we have heard him say, that this Jesus of Nazareth shall destroy this place, and shall change the customs which Moses delivered to us.

Acts 6:13-14. The fear that Jesus's followers would "change the customs which Moses delivered to us" was at the heart of their concerns. Stephen's accusers were mainly concerned that Stephen was encouraging people—with some success—to reject their traditional impression of God, and replace it with something new. They saw Stephen as someone who was blasphemously attacking the Torah itself.

The Jewish religious leaders gave Stephen a chance to explain himself, which he did. *Acts 7:1-53*. However, the leaders were not convinced that Stephen was anything more than a blasphemer. *Acts 7:57*. They "cast him out of the city, and stoned him: and the witnesses laid down their clothes at a young man's feet, whose name was Saul." *Acts 7:58*.

Stephen became known as Christianity's first martyr. In the Catholic Church, his feast day is December 26th.

Just before he was stoned to death, Stephen told the Jewish leaders that—despite their fondness for the Mosaic law—they were not keeping the law. He described at length their history as written in the Scriptures beginning with the days of Abraham. He said that their fathers had persecuted every prophet who tried to help them see God more clearly, up to and including Jesus. *Acts 7:52-53*. He essentially portrayed the Jewish people as stubborn and blind to basic truths about God. At this point, they were "cut to the heart, and they gnashed on him with their teeth." *Acts 7:54*.

The whole time that Stephen was speaking, Paul was standing there listening intently. Stephen's words, no doubt, had a big impact on Paul. Paul would go on to spread the exact same message that he had heard from Stephen on that day. Stephen may very well have been Paul's biggest influence. On that day, though, Paul was in agreement with the decision to execute Stephen. *Acts 8:1*.

When Stephen was killed, Scripture tells us that

> at that time there was a great persecution against the church which was at Jerusalem; and they were all scattered abroad throughout the regions of Judaea and Samaria, except the apostles.

Acts 8:1. Paul admitted to becoming one of the leading persecutors of the church at that time when he wrote that "beyond measure I persecuted the church of God." *Galatians 1:13*.

One day, Paul, "yet breathing out threatenings and slaughter against the disciples of the Lord, went unto the high priest." *Acts 9:1*. He asked the high priest to write him letters authorizing him to go "to Damascus to the synagogues, that if he found any of this way, whether they were men or women, he might bring them bound unto Jerusalem." *Acts 9:2*.

While on his way to Damascus, he famously had an experience with the Risen Christ.

> And as he journeyed, he came near Damascus: and suddenly there shined round about him a light from heaven: And he fell to the earth, and heard a voice saying unto him, Saul, Saul, why persecutest thou me? And he said, Who art thou, Lord? And the Lord said, I am Jesus who thou persecutest.

Acts 9:3-5. Paul wrote of his conversion experience that

> when it pleased God, who separated me from my
> mother's womb, and called me by his grace, To reveal
> his Son in me, that I might preach him among the hea-
> then; immediately I conferred not with flesh and blood:
> Neither went I up to Jerusalem to them which were
> apostles before me; but I went into Arabia, and re-
> turned again unto Damascus.

Galatians 1:15-17. While Scripture describes Paul's encounter with Christ as an external one on the road to Damascus, Paul himself describes his conversion as an internal one when he said that God revealed "his Son in me." Paul speaks of his impression of Christ.

Paul—very quickly after his conversion—began to preach his message about Jesus without so much as checking in with any of the apostles. Not only that, he declared himself to be an apostle of Jesus without authority or approval from any of the apostles in Jerusalem. In doing so, he claimed that God and Jesus had put him on equal footing with the Twelve Apostles—including Peter, James, and John. *1 Corinthians 1:1; 2 Corinthians 1:1; Galatians 1:1*. This did not go over very well with the Twelve Apostles, at least not at first.

Paul's contact with Jesus's original apostles was, by Paul's own account, very minimal. After his conversion, he waited three years before meeting any of the original apostles. He met with Peter and stayed with him for fifteen days. *Galatians 1:18*. Paul wrote that, during that visit, he didn't meet with any of the other apostles except for Jesus's brother James. *Galatians 1:19*. Paul didn't visit any of the original apostles again for some fourteen years. *Galatians 2:1*. That should tell you how well that first visit went. During those fourteen years, Paul openly preached his impression of the gospel, which he claimed to have learned directly from God through Christ. Paul, however, was surely influenced by the sermon he heard from Stephen just before Stephen was killed. *Acts 7:1-53*. Paul's second and final visit with the original apostles, after the fourteen-year interim, resulted in a clash, the results of which would define the way that the gospel of Christ would be preached in the Christian churches throughout the world and throughout history.

There was a standoff between Peter and *his* impression of the gospel, against Paul and *his* impression. Even though Paul never met Jesus—and only had two brief visits with Jesus's original apostles—Paul's impression of the gospel would quickly prevail while Peter's version of it would die on the vine.

Peter was the man whom Jesus himself had personally appointed the leader of all of the apostles. *Matthew 16:18.* For this reason, the Catholic Church considers Peter to have been the first pope. Nevertheless, Paul—who had never met Jesus in person, and was a post-Resurrection convert to Christianity after having been a major persecutor of the church—brags that, in a dispute over whether Gentile Christians needed to be circumcised, he told Peter "to his face" that he was wrong. *Galatians 2:11.*

At the time, Peter was demanding that Gentile Christians be circumcised, i.e. convert to Judaism. *Galatians 2:14.* Peter essentially believed that, since Jesus was the Jewish Messiah, any Gentiles who wished to follow Jesus must first be circumcised, i.e., convert to Judaism, and then follow Jesus, the Jewish Messiah, as converted Jews. This was Peter's vision of the church. When Paul openly disagreed with him, Peter must have been thinking, "The audacity! Who *is* this guy?"[2]

This "guy" was a man who was going by his *own* impression of God, based on his perceived personal revelation from Jesus. Paul had made a complete 180-degree turn. He went from persecuting the church because they didn't accept *his* impression of God and the Mosaic law, to someone who openly rejected the applicability of the Mosaic law when he would go on to say that circumcision means nothing. *1 Corinthians 7:19; Galatians 5:6.*

Paul didn't rely on the original apostles to tell him how to preach the gospel. Paul almost never quoted Jesus when he preached. It isn't clear how much Paul even actually knew about Jesus of Nazareth. In his epistles, he only quoted Jesus on two occasions: (1) When he taught people how to celebrate the Eucharist, *1 Corinthians 11:24-25*, and (2) when he briefly quoted what he claimed Jesus said to him in a private revelation, *2 Corinthians 12:9.*

During their last visit together, Peter and Paul came to a gentlemen's agreement. Peter permitted Paul to have an apostleship to the Gentiles which would not require them to be circumcised or otherwise follow the Mosaic law. *Galatians 2:7-9*. Peter agreed to preach only to Jews in his "apostleship of the circumcision." *Galatians 2:8*. Peter's calling was to get as many Jews as he could to follow Jesus and become Christians. Well, we all know how *that* turned out. So, Paul wins. This *one* man, who never met Jesus, and barely knew the original apostles—with his *own impression* of God, Christ, and the gospel—singlehandedly shaped the way the gospel of Jesus would be preached and taught in churches all over the world for the following millennia. The Church became a Gentile institution which, to this day—despite the fact that Jesus and the Twelve Apostles were all Jewish—does not follow the Mosaic law, most notably its provision requiring circumcision, and does not observe any of the Jewish traditions or holy days. Paul's impression of the gospel became...*the* gospel.

***

It is not an exaggeration to say that Paul rejected large portions of the Torah. Paul likened the Mosaic covenant to slavery. *Galatians 4:24*. Paul repeatedly said that circumcision means nothing. *1 Corinthians 7:19*; *Galatians 5:6*. In saying that circumcision means nothing, Paul was taking a swipe at the entire Mosaic covenant—which was referred to as the covenant of circumcision. *Genesis 17:10*.

Regarding the covenant of circumcision, Paul definitely came across as someone who had an axe to grind. He referred to circumcision as mutilation. *Philippians 3:2*. Paul went so far as to make the crass remark that those who are so fond of circumcision should go all the way and castrate themselves. *Galatians 5:12*. He accused those who wished to impose circumcision of doing it out of wanting to appear more pious. *Galatians 6:12-13*.

Paul's statements about circumcision were a serious assault on Judaism. The Jewish leaders considered Paul's comments to be a slap in the face to everything they believed in. In Scripture, God's command to circumcise goes back to the days of Abraham. *Genesis 17:10-14*. In the Scripture, God refers to the covenant of circumcision as "an everlasting covenant." *Genesis 17:13*. It is clear it was meant to be permanent.

So, is Paul saying that God made circumcision an everlasting covenant and then changed his mind? ...No. In fact, Paul must have known that Scripture clearly says that God is not a man that he should lie or change his mind. *1 Samuel 15:29*. No, Paul was making the radical assertion that circumcision was not of God from the get go. He was saying that the impression of God upon which the entire Mosaic covenant is based was off. The covenant was based on faulty impressions of God. For Jews, who lived their lives by this covenant, these were fighting words.

Paul said that the Mosaic law traumatized people by producing wrath. *Romans 4:15*. The only thing the law accomplished, according to Paul, was to show people how sinful they are, but without providing a way for people to find justification in the sight of God. *Romans 3:20*. The law simply made people feel guilty, inadequate, and worthless without remedy.

Paul had negative things to say about every aspect of the Mosaic covenant. Paul said that observing holy days, months, times, and years, was being in bondage to the Mosaic law. *Galatians 4:10*. Paul taught that people shouldn't let anyone judge them regarding what they eat and when, or whether they observe certain holy days or the sabbath. *Colossians 2:16*. What the religious leaders referred to as holy obligations of the law, Paul referred to as human precepts and teachings, and the commandments and doctrines of men. *Colossians 2:20-22*. Paul flat out referred to the Mosaic covenant as "the ministration of death." *2 Corinthians 3:7*.

Paul said that the Mosaic law worked against people when he wrote that Jesus, by his Crucifixion, "blott[ed] out the handwriting of ordinances that was against us, which was contrary to us." *Colossians 2:14*.

Paul points out that—while supposedly observing the Mosaic covenant—the Jewish religious leaders killed Jesus and pretty much every prophet who came before him who tried to repair their broken impressions of God. *1 Thessalonians 2:15 (See also Matthew 5:12)*. Paul had previously heard Stephen make this exact same point. *Acts 7:52*.

As did Jesus, Paul supplants the Mosaic covenant with one simple maxim: "Thou shalt love thy neighbour as thyself." *Romans 13:9*. (To be fair, though, this maxim *is* in the Torah. *Leviticus 19:18*.) Paul's message was that people are free to have a relationship with God, relying on their *own* impressions of God, without being slavishly bonded to the impressions of God of others—including the impressions of God of the authors of Scripture.

Jesus was gentle and respectful of the people and their beliefs when he preached. Paul, however, just sort of blurted things out in a very blunt way. But both men, though, preached the same message—first Jesus, then Paul—that the people's image and impressions of the Abrahamic/Mosaic God had done a disservice to them for a very long time.

As did Jesus before him, Paul encouraged people to use their own consciences rather than rely on literal readings of the Mosaic law. He urged people to embrace this new found freedom. Paul referred to this as "the glorious liberty of the children of God." *Romans 8:21*. However, the one caveat that Paul admonished everyone to observe is that people should not use their freedom to go by their own impressions of God as a rationalization for licentiousness. *Galatians 5:13-14*. There are things that are universally agreed upon as immoral and wrong. Paul provides a brief list of such things. *Galatians 5:19-21*.

It should be noted that Paul wasn't singling out Judaism for attack. He also made enemies of the Greeks and Romans by going around preaching that the Greco-Roman gods did not exist. *Acts 19:26*. It, no doubt, took a great deal of bravery for those gentiles to come forward and say no to worshipping the non-existent Greek and Roman gods or the emperors as gods. All of the people who came forward to follow Jesus and Paul were men and women of courage and conviction.

***

Paul would probably be the first to say that no one should just blindly accept what *he* says either. Similar to what Jesus said before him, *Luke 12:57*, Paul told people to "judge ye what I say." *1 Corinthians 10:15*. He respected the right of individuals to discern for themselves what is right.

Paul never claimed to have an exclusive direct line to God. He believed that God spoke to him, but he also believed that God spoke to everyone. Paul told people that "as touching brotherly love ye need not that I write unto you: for ye yourselves are taught of God to love one another." *1 Thessalonians 4:9*. How many religious leaders would make such a candid admission today?

Paul admitted that he was once an enemy of God. *Romans 5:10-11.* In those days when he was terrorizing people who refused to accept the impressions of God that he insisted they accept—he saw himself as an advocate for God, but he later saw that he was one of God's enemies. He owned up to the fact that he was traumatizing people in God's name.

Paul, however, went on to respect those under his ministry. He did not browbeat them. He did not expect them to accept everything he said with the uncritical naïveté of gullible children. In fact, he encouraged them to give up childish thinking and to reason like mature adults. *1 Corinthians 13:11.* He encouraged his followers to "[p]rove all things; hold fast that which is good." *1 Thessalonians 5:21.* Regarding what to believe about God, Paul said, "Let every man be fully persuaded in his own mind." *Romans 14:5.* We don't hear this in too many churches today. We don't hear preachers telling people that they can decide their own truths for themselves.

Both Jesus and Paul riled up the powers that be to kill them for the same reason. They both told people that they are free to believe in, and rely upon, the impression of God that is formed by their own consciences. This was their message of freedom—a liberating education. The authorities of their day, both Roman and Jewish, considered Jesus and then Paul to be threats to their authority. Both were executed by Roman leaders and Jewish leaders working in tandem. These mutual enemies joined forces against Jesus and Paul. Someone once said that the enemy of my enemy is my friend.

***

After having been raised to believe that his people were God's chosen people, Paul went on to teach that everyone has equal value before God. He said that "there is no respect of persons with God." *Romans 2:11.* God treats everyone equally. God does not secretly reveal himself to one group but not the other. Paul believed that God revealed himself to him, but he also respected that God spoke to everyone. All people have the law of God written in their hearts. *Romans 2:14-29.* God does not discriminate based on race or ethnicity, social status, or gender. *Galatians 3:28.* That which may be known about God is self-evident and made manifest to everyone. *Romans 1:19.* Paul encouraged all to seek the gift of prophecy, because he believed that everyone potentially has a word from God to share. *1 Corinthians 14:5.*

Paul taught that all are the temple of God—both individually and collectively. *1 Corinthians 3:16.* God doesn't just dwell out there somewhere in the heavens. God dwells within us all. He is an immanent God.

***

The freedom to follow one's own conscience is central to Paul's message—which echoes Jesus's message. Paul asked "why is my liberty judged of another man's conscience?" *1 Corinthians 10:29.* We should all ask the same question about ourselves.

Paul considered his preaching and teaching to be the testimony of his own conscience. *2 Corinthians 1:12.* He presented his teachings "to every man's conscience in the sight of God." *2 Corinthians 4:2.* In other words, Paul presented his teachings to his churches for their review and approval by their own consciences. Paul did not consider himself to be above the scrutiny and questioning of the members of his churches.

Paul taught that we can exercise our freedom to individually live according to our own personal beliefs about God. If exercising this freedom ruffles the feathers of others in our faith communities—and we'd rather not deal with the pushback—Paul said we can just keep our personal beliefs to ourselves, just between us and God. *Romans 14:22.* It's okay to do that.

***

Paul says that all of the inherited generational trauma—which he refers to as sin—came into the world through Adam, and spread from there. *Romans 5:12.* However, we can break the cycle of generational trauma, and the maladaptive behaviors (sins) that go with it, by realizing that we are liberated from the slavery of our former impressions of God, and are now free under God's grace. *Romans 6:14.*

Grace means unearned favor. Paul believed that people are "saved" by God because God loves us, and not because of anything good that we do. *Ephesians 2:8-9.* God's grace is a free gift. We just need to accept it.

My own relationship with God consists of simply accepting this free gift. I look at it this way: If God loves me, my eternal destiny (whatever God may have in store for me) will be fine. If God doesn't love me, then what chance do I have? Paul encouraged people to stand in this grace. *Romans 5:2*. What he meant was—to paraphrase a popular set of memes—"Relax and rest in God's grace." There is really nothing else we can do anyway.

Paul admitted that he still struggled with maladaptive behaviors that were probably trauma-induced. For Paul, the law simply pointed out to him just how sinful and traumatized he really was. On the one hand, Paul wanted to see the Mosaic law as a good and holy thing. On the other hand, he saw the law as something which created an inner struggle within himself that he hated.

> What shall we say then? Is the law sin? God forbid. Nay, I had not known sin, but by the law: for I had not known lust, except the law had said, Thou shalt not covet. But sin, taking occasion by the commandment, wrought in me all manner of concupiscence. For without the law sin was dead. For I was alive without the law once: but when the commandment came, sin revived, and I died. And the commandment, which was ordained to life, I found to be unto death. For sin, taking occasion by the commandment, deceived me, and by it slew me. Wherefore the law is holy, and the commandment holy, and just, and good. Was then that which is good made death unto me? God forbid. But sin, that it might appear sin, working death in me by that which is good; that sin by the commandment might become exceeding sinful. For we know that the law is spiritual: but I am carnal, sold under sin. For that which I do I allow not: for what I would, that do I not; but what I hate, that do I. If then I do that which I would not, I consent unto the law that it is good. Now then it is no more I that do it, but sin that dwelleth in me. For I know that in me (that is, in my flesh,) dwelleth no good thing: for to will is present with me;

but how to perform that which is good I find not. For the good that I would I do not: but the evil which I would not, that I do. Now if I do that I would not, it is no more I that do it, but sin that dwelleth in me. I find then a law, that, when I would do good, evil is present with me. For I delight in the law of God after the inward man: But I see another law in my members, warring against the law of my mind, and bringing me into captivity to the law of sin which is in my members. O wretched man that I am! who shall deliver me from the body of this death? I thank God through Jesus Christ our Lord. So then with the mind I myself serve the law of God; but with the flesh the law of sin.

Romans 7:7-25. Paul contrasted living "in the flesh," which is succumbing to all of our trauma-induced behaviors, with living "in the spirit," which is living in the freedom of rising above our trauma-induced issues which—in Paul's view—can only be accomplished with the help of God. *Romans 8:1-13*.

***

I like Paul. He comes across as very relatable to me. If offered the proverbial choice of which one of the apostles I would like to sit down and have a beer with, my choice would be Paul, hands down. His writings make it seem as if he was a plain talker and a straight shooter. He wasn't above using saucy language, even in his epistles to his churches. For example, Paul wrote:

> I count all things but loss for the excellency of the knowledge of Christ Jesus my Lord; for whom I have suffered the loss of all things, and do count them but dung, that I may win Christ.

Philippians 3:8. The Greek word for "dung" used in this passage by Paul is σκύβαλον (pronounced *skubalon*).[3] It is a harsh word which can also be legitimately translated as "shit." You've gotta love Paul.

Paul also seems to have been a sports enthusiast. Paul encouraged his protégé, Timothy, to "[f]ight the good fight of faith." *1 Timothy 6:12*. Paul analogized his preparations for preaching the gospel to the way a boxer trains for a fight. He said,

> so fight I, not as one that beateth the air: But I keep
> under my body, and bring it into subjection: lest that
> by any means, when I have preached to others, I myself
> should be a castaway.

1 Corinthians 9:26-27. It appears Paul knew a thing or two about boxing. Paul also made similar analogies about running. *1 Corinthians 9:24; Galatians 5:7; Philippians 3:13-14; 2 Timothy 4:8*. Even though most biblical scholars do not believe that Paul authored the book of Hebrews in the New Testament, there is a reference to running in that book which might indicate Pauline authorship after all. It says "let us run with patience the race that is set before us." *Hebrews 12:1*. Paul definitely seems like someone I would have liked to have known.

***

As did Jesus, Paul targets the family as the source of most of the inherited generational trauma. Reiterating the reparenting message of Jesus, Paul encourages us to embrace the freedom we can have by reaching out to our heavenly father. *Romans 8:15*. Paul also offers himself, to the churches he founded, as a father figure. *1 Corinthians 4:15*. He encouraged people to follow his lead and example. *1 Corinthians 4:16, 11:1*. He did not intend to replace the heavenly Father. But, in saying that he became their father, he offered some assistance in the reparenting process that Jesus intended.

As previously discussed, Jesus seemed to advocate a radical redefinition of family as the solution to generational trauma. *Matthew 12:46-50*. Paul seemed to have a less radical approach. Unwilling to give up on the family, Paul wrote the following to children and parents, which he offered as a solution to generational trauma.

> Children, obey your parents in the Lord: for this is
> right. Honour thy father and mother; (which is the first

commandment with promise;) That it may be well with thee, and thou mayest live long on the earth. And, ye fathers, provoke not your children to wrath: but bring them up in the nurture and admonition of the Lord.

Ephesians 6:1-4. Paul telling children to honor their father and mother comes from the Ten Commandments given to Moses on Mount Sinai. *Exodus 20:12.* So he apparently didn't think the Mosaic Law was *all* bad.

In the society in which Paul grew up and lived—as well as the Mosaic law—children had no rights to speak of within the family. Scripture advocates the use of corporal punishment. *Proverbs 13:24.* Under the Mosaic law, rebellious and disobedient children were guilty of a capital offense—actually risking the death penalty.

If a man have a stubborn and rebellious son, which will not obey the voice of his father, or the voice of his mother, and that, when they have chastised him, will not hearken unto them: Then shall his father and his mother lay hold on him, and bring him out unto the elders of his city, and unto the gate of his place; And they shall say unto the elders of his city, This our son is stubborn and rebellious, he will not obey our voice; he is a glutton, and a drunkard. And all the men of his city shall stone him with stones, that he die: so shalt thou put evil away from among you; and all Israel shall hear, and fear.

Deuteronomy 21:18-21. The way to deal with a stubborn and rebellious son, was to have him killed! That's what it says, right there in the Mosaic law.

Children were to respect and obey their parents in all things. But Paul taught that respect and honor between parents and children works both ways. Paul told fathers to "provoke not your children to wrath." *Ephesians 6:4.* Perhaps this stemmed from Paul's own experience as a child. Did his parents provoke him to wrath? What I would give to have that beer with Paul.

Paul also taught: "Rebuke not an elder, but intreat him as a father; and the younger men as brethren; The elder women as mothers; the younger as sisters, with all purity." *1 Timothy 5:1-2*. This is similar to what Jesus said, expanding the definition of family, that "whosoever shall do the will of my Father which is in heaven, the same is my brother, and sister, and mother." *Matthew 12:50*.

For Paul, this is how you do it. This is how you strive to end generational trauma. You start within the family, the source of much of the trauma. You teach your children non-trauma-inducing impressions of God. And you teach them to think for themselves. You tell them, as they grow, it's okay for them to form their *own* impressions of God. It's okay for them to use their *own* consciences. And when the children occasionally get things wrong—which they inevitably will (because they're not perfect like you)—don't make them feel like dirt.

I know, all of this is easier said than done. God knows I haven't been a perfect parent. It's difficult not to pass along our own trauma to our children. And our children won't be perfect either. But together, with the Sermon on the Mount God's help, we can work to fix all of this. Regarding this, Scripture says, "Train up a child in the way he should go: and when he is old, he will not depart from it." *Proverbs 22:6*.

***

In around 64/65 A.D., Paul went on to give his life for the message of freedom that he preached to his churches. Paul shares a feast day on June 29th with St. Peter.

AFTERWORD

THE FAMILY IS where children form their first impressions of the world around them. For families of faith, it is also where children form their very first impressions of God. My father always said that the family is everyone's first church. Some of my earliest memories are of my parents taking my sister and I to Sunday Mass at our local parish, which my parents taught us was "Jesus's house."

My childhood education took place at our local Catholic parochial elementary school. I put in my eight years. I do look back fondly at those days. When it came to the religion lessons, they kept it simple. They taught me all of the pleasant, loving, and uplifting things about God and Jesus. They did a good job.

They also taught lessons about Noah's Ark, Moses and the plagues and such. They put a positive spin on these stories for us children. Somehow, they managed to make us feel good about all those people being killed by God. It's funny but, the fact that those events involved God killing so many people just seemed to go right over my head. ...Or did it?

I don't recall feeling traumatized by God at the time. But maybe the damage that I sustained was that I simply casually believed that God had a good reason for killing all those people. That if God flooded everyone in the world, it's because it needed to be done. That if God killed all of the firstborn sons in Egypt, it's probably because they deserved it. If God did it, then it must have been the right thing to do. Killing lots of people is just one of the things that God did. That was all there was to it. I didn't know my inner Genesis 18 Abraham at the time.

Throughout my childhood, one of my staples was making sure to watch Cecil B. DeMille's 1956 *The Ten Commandments* every year when it came on television during the Passover/Easter holy season. As a child, I was drawn to that movie like a moth to a flame. It was definitely must watch TV for me. I remember feeling like the film had a horror movie quality to it. And what kid didn't love a good horror flick? The voice of God in *The Ten Commandments* was just downright frightening. Particularly when God spoke during the burning bush scene and when God gave the Commandments to Moses on Mount Sinai. That was some scary stuff right there. Loved it.

It was, of course, also scary when all of those soldiers and their horses drowned in the Red Sea. It was scary too when all those screams were heard throughout Egypt when the firstborn sons were dying in every household. And the deaths of the firstborn was preceded by the appearance of this very ominous looking black cloud along with the ominous sounding music to go with it. The movie made it seem that—when he was going to start killing people—God definitely had a flair for the dramatic. Like tens of millions of other people, I grew up as a child absorbing these visuals over and over again. I accepted the entire movie as fact. This is God. This is what he did. This is how he is. *The Ten Commandments* is one of the top ten money grossing movies of all time.[1] That's a lot of people absorbing the same visuals as I did.

No, neither my parents, nor my Catholic elementary school, meant to instill traumatizing impressions of God within me. They meant well. And, for the most part, they did a great job of educating me. They inadvertently and unconsciously passed along whatever generational trauma they experienced, and whatever traumatic impressions of God they may have inherited, because that's what we *all* do. We can't help it. We're only human.

I can't speak to what DeMille was thinking. But today I realize that, when we watch *The Ten Commandments*, we are seeing the Abrahamic/Mosaic God as filtered through DeMille. The movie is largely Cecil B. DeMille's impression of God.

***

Jesus and Paul were both executed simply for telling people that—despite his inscrutability—God can be known. God has placed all that we need to know about him in our hearts and in our minds. To find God, we only need to look within. And that goes for all of us. He gave us consciences which we can and should use to discern God's will. We don't need to be taught about God. We already know.

The human mind is *very* powerful. It is way more powerful than most of us realize. Every single reality around us—those things made by human beings—was inspired first by human thought. Every successful venture started out as someone's idea. Sometimes these ideas seemed crazy and undoable. But yet, they worked. Our invisible thoughts become visible realities. We can say that about every single invention or innovation. We can say that about every single piece of artwork. We can say that about every single thing that was ever created through human effort—every written thing, everything that was ever built, every problem ever solved, every disease ever cured, every scientific achievement, every religion or philosophy. All of it. Every visible reality started out as someone's invisible thought.

That's power.

People filled with skepticism and pessimism often say, "I'll believe it when I see it." But, in keeping with how the subconscious mind operates, Jesus tells us: "You'll see it when you believe it." *Mark 11:24.*

The human mind, according to Scripture, can also be deceptive and desperately wicked. *Jeremiah 17:9.* Unfortunately, the most horrific, cruel, murderous, insane acts ever committed by humans also begin as invisible thoughts and ideas. Whenever we learn about any human atrocity—and they happen every day—know that it started out as just a thought or idea hatched in someone's twisted mind. Yet, as twisted as some people may be, they can still bring their evil ideas to fruition.

We know today that most of what goes on in our minds happens at a subconscious level.[2] Our subconscious minds have deceptively convinced us that we have no control over it, convinced us to say and do things that go directly against our best interests, convinced us to cause pain and harm to ourselves and others. Our subconscious minds operate stealthily in the background causing us to be largely unaware of its existence.

Our subconscious minds have convinced us that every negative thing that our own minds have created—including every situation and circumstance—are just happening to us because of reasons beyond our control. It's as if our subconscious mind creates these negative circumstances for us in our lives and then turns around and tells us, "Don't look at me! I've got nothing to do with this mess." We then blame God or others for these circumstances when, in fact, we caused and orchestrated them ourselves.

We *choose* to be addicted, we *choose* to be depressed, we *choose* to have and embrace fear and anxiety, we *choose* to do harm, we *choose* to hate, we *choose* to ruin our own lives. And yes, we *choose* to be traumatized. These are all choices. Subconscious choices. And when we say, "No! It's not me! I'm not choosing this! I can't change my circumstances!" That's us believing our subconscious mind's lies. To which Jesus might respond, "O ye of little faith." *Matthew 6:30.* We can truly be our own worst enemy.[3] Our subconscious minds *are us.* In the end, if we suffer from trauma, it's because we are traumatizing ourselves.

Our *subconscious* minds remember every single experience we've ever had. Every little bit of it. Our *conscious* minds may repress some memories.[4] But our *subconscious* minds never forget.[5] Ever. Our subconscious minds teach us how to deal with any disturbing memories. It is the subconscious that comes up with our coping mechanisms. Conscious mind or subconscious mind—it's all *us.*

Our subconscious minds are very suggestible, especially the subconscious minds of children. During childhood, the subconscious mind uncritically believes whatever people may say about us. It absorbs and believes all of the negative messages it receives about us. It lets the negative opinions that others have about us define us. As a result of this, our subconscious mind provides us with internal thoughts disguised as external realities. "You're worthless and unworthy!" "You're a big failure!" "Everyone hates you and God hates you too!" Our own subconscious minds can operate like a big bully who convinces us that it has all the power. An enemy that wants to run—or should I say ruin—our lives. What's that famous line from the *Pogo* cartoon strip? "We have met the enemy and he is us."[6] This attack on our conscious minds by our subconscious minds is what Scripture refers to when it says that being double minded can interfere with our relationship with God. *James 1:8.*

In reality, our conscious minds can have the power over our subconscious minds. We may just not know it—yet. Jesus said, "Behold, I give unto you power to tread on serpents and scorpions, and over all the power of the enemy: and nothing shall by any means hurt you." *Luke 10:19.*

Afterword

Our own subconscious minds convince us to blame some external force for our evil thoughts and temptations. We can blame Satan like he's some tormenting boogie man out to ruin us when, in fact, we are our own enemy. Who needs a devil when we already have a subconscious mind that is evil and deceptive above all things working against us? *Jeremiah 17:9.*

> Let no man say when he is tempted, I am tempted of God: for God cannot be tempted with evil, neither tempteth he any man: But every man is tempted, when he is drawn away of his own lust, and enticed.

James 1:13-14. Notice it doesn't say here that we are drawn away by the devil. It says we are drawn away by our "own lust." That is, we are drawn away from God by our own selves.

We need to take ownership of our own minds—both conscious and subconscious. It's us. We're doing this to ourselves. Let's stop.

***

Many people don't realize how much guidance the Bible provides us on getting ourselves in the right frame of mind. It's not just about our souls in the ever after. It's about our minds here and now.

Belonging to a faith community can and should be a wonderful thing. If you belong to such a community and you choose to abide by its rituals, obligations, and tradition, that can be great, as long as it's *your* choice and in conformity with *your* conscience. But remember—don't let anyone else's impression of God traumatize you. You own your conscience. You own your subconscious mind. You have the power. You have the freedom to worship and pray to your own impression of God, if that is what your conscience tells you to do. Don't let anybody take that away from you. There are people who gave their lives just to let you know the extent of your power and freedom within.

***

Towards the end of the 1939 MGM motion picture, *The Wizard of Oz*, Dorothy says to Glinda, the Good Witch, "Oh, will you help me? Can

189

you help me?" To which Glinda replies, "You don't need to be helped any longer. You've always had the power to go back to Kansas." Dorothy asks, "I have?" The Scarecrow asks, "Then why didn't you tell her before?" Then Glinda says, "Because she wouldn't have believed me. She had to learn it for herself." Many people, when told that they have the power within themselves to change their lives, refuse to believe it. Don't be one of them. You can use your power within to change your life. That power was given to you by God. That power *is* God. *Acts 1:8*.

Jesus, then Paul, were executed for doing nothing more than telling people that they have the power within them to overcome and rise above the inherited generational trauma that holds them back, keeps them down, and blocks them from becoming the blessed human beings that God intended them to be. We all have the power within us to be the authentic selves that God created us to be.

You. You have that power. Use it.

Where you go with all of this is your choice. As people often say today—you do you. As Paul of Tarsus said regarding what we believe about God, "Let every man be persuaded in his own mind." *Romans 14:5*. As for me, I pray to, and put my faith in, the God as presented by Jesus in the Sermon on the Mount.

NOTES

PREFACE
1. Martha Henriques
   "Can the Legacy of Trauma Be Passed Down the Generations?"
   The British Broadcasting Corporation – March 26, 2019
   https://www.BBC.com/future/article/20190326-what-is-epigenetics
2. Andrew Curry
   "Parents' Emotional Trauma May Change Their Children's Biology"
   American Association for the Advancement of Science – July 18, 2019
   https://www.Science.org/content/article/parents-emotional-trauma-may-change-their-children-s-biology-studies-mice-show-how
3. Jennifer Rosenberg
   "Sigmund Freud: The Father of Psychoanalysis"
   Dotdash Meredith – Updated January 22, 2020
   https://www.ThoughtCo.com/sigmund-freud-1779806
4. John Fletcher
   "Freud and the Scene of Trauma"
   Fordham University Press – December 2, 2013
   https://books.Google.com/books/about/
   Freud_and_the_Scene_of_Trauma.html?id=R1GoDwAAQBAJ

CHAPTER ONE
1. N.K. Sanders
   "Epic of Gilgamesh"
   Assyrian International News Agency
   Books Online
   http://www.AINA.org/books/eog/eog.pdf
2. Louise M. Pryke
   "The Influence of Gilgamesh on the Bible"
   Hebrew, Biblical, and Jewish Studies
   Sydney University – November 2019
   https://bibleinterp.Arizona.edu/articles/influence-gilgamesh-bible
3. Joshua J. Mark
   "Ur"
   World History Encyclopedia
   https://www.WorldHistory.org/ur/
4. *"Existentialism"*
   Stanford Encyclopedia of Philosophy

https://plato.Stanford.edu/entries/existentialism/

5. Hope Gillette
"What's an Existential Crisis and How Can I Overcome It?"
PsychCentral
Healthline Media
https://PsychCentral.com/lib/existential-crisis-and-dread

6. William Shakespeare
"As You Like It"
Act II, Scene VII, Line 139
http://www.shakespeare-online.com/plays/asu_2_7.html

7. Rachel E. Menzies, et al.
"Death Anxiety: The Worm at the Core of Mental Health"
Australian Psychological Society – December 2018
https://psychology.org.au/for-members/publications/inpsych/2018/
december-issue-6/death-anxiety-the-worm-at-the-core-of-mental-heal

8. Cynthia Vinney
"Why Do We Enjoy Horror Movies"
Verywell Mind
Dotdash Media – April 8, 2022
https://www.VeryWellmind.com/why-do-people-like-horror-movies-5224447

9. Brian McNeill
"U.S. Life Expectancy Continued to Fall in 2021"
Virginia Commonwealth University – April 7, 2022
https://www.news.VCU.edu/article/2022/04/us-life-expectancy-continued-
to-fall-in-2021

10. Nell Wing
"Origin of the Serenity Prayer: A Historical Paper"
Alcoholics Anonymous – Revised July 30, 2009
https://www.AA.org/sites/default/files/literature/assets/smf-129_en.pdf

11. Katarina Skogman Pavulans, Ph.D
"Being in Want of Control: Experiences of Being on the Road to, and Making, a Suicide Attempt"
International Journal of Qualitative Studies on Health and Well-Being – May 3, 2012
https://www.ncbi.nlm.NIH.gov/pmc/articles/PMC3345936/

12. *"Who Wrote Ecclesiastes and What Does It Mean?"*
Zondervan Academic
HarperCollins Publishers – October 21, 2017
https://ZondervanAcademic.com/blog/who-wrote-ecclesiastes-and-what-
does-it-mean

13. Karel van der Toorn
"Did Ecclesiastes Copy Gilgamesh?"
Biblical Archaeology Society Online Archive
Bible Review 16:1, February 2000
https://www.BASLibrary.org/bible-review/16/1/9

Notes

CHAPTER TWO

1. *"Ancient Atomism"*
   Stanford Encyclopedia of Ancient Philosophy – Revised October 18, 2022
   Philosophy Department, Stanford University
   https://plato.Stanford.edu/entries/atomism-ancient/

CHAPTER FOUR

1. *"Dei Verbum"* Chapter III
   This 1965 document is also known as the Dogmatic Constitution on Divine
   Revelation and is part of the documents of Vatican II.
   https://www.Vatican.va/archive/hist_councils/ii_vatican_council/
   documents/vat-ii_const_19651118_dei-verbum_en.html
2. John Calvin
   "Institutes of the Christian Religion" – Chapter 4, Section 1
   Christian Classics Ethereal Library
   https://www.CCEL.org/ccel/calvin/institutes.iii.v.html
3. Ibid.
4. Ibid.
5. Ibid. Chapter 1, Section 1
6. Ibid. Chapter 4, Section 1
7. Ibid. Chapter 6, Section 1
8. Ibid.
9. Regarding knowledge of God, the observation that the most that any
   individual can achieve is a personal *impression* of God—including the authors of
   the Bible—is at the heart of the Bahá'í faith, which has some 8 million
   adherents worldwide.
   https://www.Bahai.org/
10. *"Dei Verbum"* Chapter III
    This 1965 document is also known as the Dogmatic Constitution on Divine
    Revelation and is part of the documents of Vatican II.
    https://www.Vatican.va/archive/hist_councils/ii_vatican_council/
    documents/vat-ii_const_19651118_dei-verbum_en.html
11. Ibid.
12. St. Augustine of Hippo
    "The City of God" (Book XVI) Chapter 9
    https://www.NewAdvent.org/fathers/120116.htm
13. Ibid.
14. Ibid.
15. Ibid.
16. *"Mother Teresa: A Saint Despite 'Spiritual Darkness'"*
    The Associated Press
    The Denver Post – September 1, 2016
    https://www.denverpost.com/2016/09/01/mother-teresa-a-saint-despite-
    spiritual-darkness/
17. Ibid.
18. Daniel Trotta

Notes

Pages 43 through 58

"Letters Reveal Mother Teresa's Doubt About Faith"
Reuters World News – August 24, 2007
https://www.Reuters.com/article/us-teresa-letters/letters-reveal-mother-teresas-doubt-about-faith-idUSN2435506020070824

19. Ibid.
20. Sri Swami Chidananda
    "Hinduism – Monotheism and Polytheism Reconciled"
    The Divine Life Society
    https://www.DLSHQ.org/discourse/hinduism-monotheism-and-polytheism-reconciled/
21. Liz Neporent
    "You Really Can Be Scared to Death"
    ABC News – October 24, 2012
    https://ABCnews.Go.com/Health/die-fright/story?id=17554297
22. "Filiolique"
    Catholic Encyclopedia
    New Advent
    https://www.NewAdvent.org/cathen/06073a.htm
23. *"Negative Theology (Apophatic Theology)"*
    New World Encyclopedia
    https://www.NewWorldEncyclopedia.org/entry/Negative_Theology_(Apophatic_Theology)
24. *"Thomas Aquinas, 'The Five Ways'"*
    Philosophy of Religion
    Lander University
    https://philosophy.Lander.edu/intro/aquinas.shtml

CHAPTER FIVE

1. *"Jonestown"*
   Federal Bureau of Investigation (FBI)
   https://www.FBI.gov/history/famous-cases/jonestown
2. Catechism of the Catholic Church, paragraph 1782
   http://www.SCBorromeo.org/ccc/para/1782.htm
3. Catechism of the Catholic Church, paragraph 1800
   http://www.SCBorromeo.org/ccc/para/1800.htm
4. This teaching on conscience in the Catechism of the Catholic Church stems from one of the declaration documents of the Council of Vatican II, where the teaching is explained more fully. The document is *"Dignitatis Humanae"* (Declaration on Religious Freedom) Pope Paul VI – December 7, 1965
   https://www.vatican.va/archive/hist_councils/ii_vatican_council/documents/vat-ii_decl_19651207_dignitatis-humanae_en.html
5. Catechism of the Catholic Church, paragraph 1783
   http://www.SCBorromeo.org/ccc/para/1783.htm
6. Catechism of the Catholic Church, paragraph 1857
   http://www.SCBorromeo.org/ccc/para/1857.htm
7. Elizabeth Landau

"Religious OCD: 'I'm Going to Hell'"
CNN – May 31, 2014
https://www.CNN.com/2014/05/31/health/ocd-scrupulosity-religion/index.html

8. Rachel Ehmke
    "Understanding Religious OCD: When the Motivation Is Anxiety, Not faith"
    Child Mind Institute – Reviewed and Updated October 12, 2021
    https://ChildMind.org/article/understanding-religious-ocd/

9. *The Twilight Zone*, Season 3 Episode 8, originally aired on CBS on November 3, 1961.

10. It is possible that Hezekiah was unaware of the existence of the Torah. There is a disputed theory that the Torah was lost and forgotten by the Israelites for many generations, including during the reign of Hezekiah. Some 60 years after the end of Hezekiah's reign, Scripture tells us that the original scroll of the Torah was found during a renovation of the then dilapidated Temple in Jerusalem, which had been destroyed by the Babylonians in 587/586 B.C. *2 Kings 22:8; 2 Chronicles 34:15*. Regardless, Hezekiah's impression of God was at odds with that of Moses regarding the serpent pole.

11. *"Dei Verbum"* Chapter III
    This 1965 document is also known as *The Dogmatic Constitution on Divine Revelation* and is part of the documents of Vatican II.

12. Andrew McGowan
    "How December 25 Became Christmas"
    Biblical Archaeology Society – July 23, 2022
    https://www.BiblicalArchaeology.org/daily/people-cultures-in-the-bible/jesus-historical-jesus/how-december-25-became-christmas/

13. Jimmy Akin
    "Yes, the Slaughter of the Innocents Really Happened, and Here Is the Evidence"
    Blog – National Catholic Register – December 26, 2012
    https://www.NCRegister.com/blog/did-the-slaughter-of-the-innocents-really-happen

14. *"Feast of the Holy Innocents, Martyrs"*
    Catholic Culture
    https://www.CatholicCulture.org/culture/liturgicalyear/calendar/day.cfm?date=2021-12-28

CHAPTER SIX

1. See the reference to the *Epic of Gilgamesh* in Chapter One.

2. Janelle Cox
    "Healing from Toxic Shame"
    PsychCentral – Updated May 13, 2022
    Healthline Media
    https://PsychCentral.com/lib/what-is-toxic-shame

3. Genesis 2:16-18

4. Genesis 3:11-13 reveals this pecking order. When God asks Adam and Eve if they had eaten of the forbidden fruit, Adam answers first. Adam blames, "[t]he

woman whom thou gavest to be with me." Adam blames Eve but also blames God for giving Eve to be with him as his partner. God then turns to Eve who in turn blames the serpent. Adam, then Eve, then the serpent. That is the pecking order. The serpent, as the lowest in the order, had no one whom to shift the blame.

5. Genesis 3:3
6. Genesis 3:1
7. Genesis 2:17, 3:3
8. Genesis 3:4
9. Genesis 3:5
10. Genesis 3:6
11. Genesis 3:6
12. Genesis 3:5
13. Genesis 3:22
14. Genesis 3:5
15. Lisa Fritscher
    "Understanding Fear of Abandonment"
    VeryWellMind – Updated November 13, 2022
    Dotdash Media, Inc.
    https://www.VeryWellMind.com/fear-of-abandonment-2671741
16. Christopher Bergland
    "Why Some Children Live With a Persistent Fear of Abandonment"
    Psychology Today – January 17, 2021
    https://www.PsychologyToday.com/us/blog/the-athletes-way/202101/why-some-children-live-persistent-fear-abandonment

CHAPTER SEVEN

1. David Max Eichorn
   "Cain, Son of the Serpent"
   SP Books, 1985
   https://books.Google.com/books/about/Cain_Son_of_the_Serpent.html?id=wPwEFXmjsiAC
2. Genesis 4:12
3. Genesis 4:15
4. Emma Robson
   "Sibling Blues – Causes of Sibling Rivalry and How to Handle It?"
   Parenting Square – August 11, 2022
   https://www.ParentingSquare.com/psychology/causes-of-sibling-rivalry/
5. Lawrence R. Samuel, Ph.D.
   "The Psychology of Murder"
   Psychology Today – March 12, 2022
   Sussex Publishers, LLC
   https://www.psychologytoday.com/us/blog/psychology-yesterday/202203/the-psychology-murder
6. Martin Kaste
   "Open Cases: Why One-Third of Murders in America Go Unresolved"

Notes

NPR – WNYC – March 30, 2015
https://www.NPR.org/2015/03/30/395069137/open-cases-why-one-third-of-murders-in-america-go-unresolved

7.   Chris Hacker, et al.
     "A 'Coin Flip': Nearly Half of U.S. Murders Go Unsolved as Cases Rise"
     CBS News – Updated June 29, 2022
     https://www.CBSNews.com/news/unsolved-murders-crime-without-punishment/

8.   Luke 3:36-38

CHAPTER EIGHT

1.   *"Old Testament Word No. 5162"*
     Strong's Exhaustive Concordance
     https://BibleHub.com/strongs/hebrew/5162.htm

2.   Mark R. Leary, Ph.D.
     "Emotional Responses to Interpersonal Rejection"
     National Library of Medicine – December 2015
     National Center for Biotechnology Information
     National Institutes of Health
     https://www.NCBI.NLM.NIH.gov/pmc/articles/PMC4734881/

3.   The biblical wars include the Battle of Siddim, *Genesis 14:1-24*; Crossing the Red Sea, *Exodus 13:17-15:21*; the Battle of Rephidim, *Exodus 17:8-13*; the Golden Calf Massacre, *Exodus 32:26-28*; the Conquest of Heshbon, *Numbers 21:21-31, Deuteronomy 2:24-37, Judges 11:19-23*; the Conquest of Bashan, *Numbers 21:33-35, Deuteronomy 3:1-7*; the War against the Midianites, *Numbers 31*; the Conquest of Canaan, *Joshua 2-19, Judges 1*; the Battle of Jericho, *Joshua 5:13-6:27*; the Battles of Ai, *Joshua 7-8*; the Battle of the Waters of Merom, *Joshua 11*; the Moabite Conquest of Israel, *Judges 3:12-14*; the Battle of the fords of Jordan, *Judges 3:15-30*; the Battle of Mount Tabor, *Judges 4-5*; Gideon's campaign against the Midianites, *Judges 6-8*; the Shechemite Rebellion, *Judges 9:22-57*; the Israelite-Ammonite war, *Judges 11:4-40*; the Shibboleth war, *Judges 12:1-6*; Samson versus the Philistines, *Judges 15-16*; the sack of Laish, *Judges 18:9-31*; the Battle of Gibeah, *Judges 19-21*; the Battle of Aphek, *1 Samuel 4:1-11*; the Battle of Mizpah, *1 Samuel 7:5-15*; the Siege of Jabesh-Gilead, *1 Samuel 11*; the Battle of Michmash, *1 Samuel 13-14:23*; Saul's Amalekite campaign, *1 Samuel 15:1-11*; David defeats Goliath, *1 Samuel 17:1-51*; the Foreskin war, *1 Samuel 18:12-30*; the Battle of Mount Gilboa, *1 Chronicles 10*; the Pool of Gibeon; *2 Samuel 2:12-17*; the Siege of Jebus, *2 Samuel 5:6-10, 1 Chronicles 11:4-9*; the Battle of the Wood of Ephraim, *2 Samuel 18:6-8*; the Battle of Baal-perazim, *2 Samuel 5:17-25, 1 Chronicles 14:8-17*; Jeroboam's revolt, *1 Kings 11; 2 Chronicles 13*; Shishak's sack of Jerusalem, *1 Kings 14:25-30, 2 Chronicles 12:1-12*; the Battle of Mount Zemaraim, *1 Kings 12, 2 Chronicles 13*; the Battle of Zephath, *2 Chronicles 14:8-15*; the Tibni-Omri war, *1 Kings 16:15-22*; the Israelite-Aramean war, *1 Kings 20:1-34, 2 Kings 6:8-7:16*; the Battle of Zair, *2 Kings 8:20-22, 2 Chronicles 21:8-10*; the Philistine-Arab raid on Judah, *2 Chronicles 21:12-17*; the Sack of Tiphsah, *2 Kings 15:16*; Tiglath Pileser III's conquest of

Notes
Pages 84 through 90

the Levant, *2 Kings 16:5-9*; the Syro-Ephraimite war, *2 Kings 16:5, 2 Chronicles 28, Isaiah 7:1*; the Siege of Samaria, *2 Kings 17:3-6, 2 Kings 18:9-11*; Sennacherib's campaign in the Levant, *2 Kings 18-19, Isaiah 36-37, 2 Chronicles 32*; the Siege of Lachish, *2 Kings 18, 2 Chronicles 32, Micah 1:13*; the Battle of Ninevah, *Nahum 2-3, Jonah*; the Battle of Megiddo, *2 Kings 23:29-30, 2 Chronicles 35:20-25*; the Battle of Carchemish, *Ezekiel 30, Jeremiah 46:3-12*; the Babylonian Siege of Jerusalem, *2 Kings 24:10-16*; the Babylonian destruction of Jerusalem, *2 Kings 25, 2 Chronicles 36, Lamentations 4-5, Jeremiah 32-52*; the Purim war, *Esther 9:5-16*. In addition to all of these accounts, Scripture refers to a more complete chronicle of wars in "the book of the wars of the LORD." *Numbers 21:14*. Moses referred to God as "a man of war." *Exodus 15:3*.

4. *"Old Testament Word No. 4557"*
    Strong's Exhaustive Concordance
    https://BibleHub.com/hebrew/4557.htm
5. Pamela Li
    "What Is a Dysfunctional Family & How to Break the Cycle"
    Parenting For Brain – Updated February 4, 2023
    https://www.ParentingForBrain.com/dysfunctional-family/
6. In this passage, God seems to be speaking to other gods. There are many opinions about this. The author believes this is probably the case because this story was passed down from the ancient Sumerians, who were polytheists. This book does not delve into a study of this. The reader is encouraged to research this issue if they wish.
7. In chapter three, the author discusses traumatizing impressions of God in Scripture in more detail.
8. Luke 3:34-36

CHAPTER NINE

1. Yehuda Altein
    "Who Was Terah?"
    Chabad.org
    The Chabad-Lubavitch Media Center
    https://www.Chabad.org/library/article_cdo/aid/4529921/Jewish/Who-Was-Terah.htm
2. Ibid.
3. Nissan Mindel
    "Abraham's Early Life"
    Chabad.org
    The Chabad-Lubavitch Media Center
    https://www.Chabad.org/library/article_cdo/aid/112063/Jewish/Abrahams-Early-Life.htm
4. Ibid.
5. Ibid.
6. Ibid.
7. Ibid.
8. Yehuda Altein

Notes
Pages 90 through 96

"Who Was Terah?"
Chabad.org
The Chabad-Lubavitch Media Center
https://www.Chabad.org/library/article_cdo/aid/4529921/Jewish/Who-Was-Terah.htm

9. Ibid.
10. Ibid.
11. It should be noted that the Qur'an cites Ishmael as the rightful firstborn son of Abraham, not Isaac.
12. Christian scholars interpret this as a foreshadow of Jesus, the "Lamb of God," who would go on to be sacrificed by his Father on the Cross.
13. Richard Lettieri, Ph.D.
"Why Would a Parent Kill Their Own Child?"
Psychology Today – April 27, 2021
https://www.PsychologyToday.com/us/blog/decoding-madness/202104/why-would-parent-kill-their-own-child
14. *"Compulsive Lying"*
GoodTherapy – Updated May 8, 2018
https://www.GoodTherapy.org/blog/psychpedia/compulsive-lying
15. Darius Cikanavicius
"Childhood Trauma: How We Learn to Lie, Hide, and Be Inauthentic"
PsychCentral – August 13, 2018
Healthline Media
https://PsychCentral.com/blog/psychology-self/2018/08/trauma-hiding#1
16. Ibid.
17. David Hosier, MSc
"Pathological Lying: Its Link To Childhood Trauma"
Childhood Trauma Recovery
https://ChildhoodTraumaRecovery.com/blog/pathological-lying-its-link-to-childhood-trauma/
18. Darius Cikanavicius
"Childhood Trauma: How We Learn to Lie, Hide, and Be Inauthentic"
PsychCentral – August 13, 2018
Healthline Media
https://PsychCentral.com/blog/psychology-self/2018/08/trauma-hiding#1
19. Ibid.
20. Ibid.
21. Ibid.
22. Ibid.
23. Ibid.
24. *"Ishmael"*
Jewish Encyclopedia
The Kopelman Foundation
https://www.JewishEncyclopedia.com/articles/8251-ishmael

199

25. According to Scripture, Abraham was 86 years old when Ishmael was born. *Genesis 16:16*. Abraham was 100 years old when Isaac was born. *Genesis 21:5*. Therefore, Ishmael was 14 years old when Isaac was born.
26. Genesis 21:9-10
27. Genesis 21:9-14
28. Genesis 22:1-19
29. Genesis 22:7
30. Genesis 22:8
31. Genesis 22:10
32. Genesis 22:11-12
33. Genesis 22:13
34. Genesis 22:11
35. No conversations between Abraham and Isaac are recorded in the Bible after this incident.

CHAPTER TEN

1. Ted Boscia
   "Study: Moms' Favoritism Tied to Depression in Adulthood"
   Cornell Chronicle – June 24, 2010
   Cornell University
   https://news.Cornell.edu/stories/2010/06/moms-favoritism-tied-depression-grown-children
2. Malachi 1:2-3
3. Romans 9:13
4. Genesis 25:23
5. Morgan Mandriota
   "How Being Unloved in Childhood May Affect You as an Adult"
   PsychCentral – Updated October 19, 2021
   Healthline Media
   https://PsychCentral.com/health/unloved-in-childhood-common-effects-on-your-adult-self

CHAPTER ELEVEN

1. The name Israel has been translated several different ways including "he wrestles with God," "Prince of God," "he struggles with God," and several others.
   https://KingJamesBibleDictionary.com/StrongsNo/H3478/Israel
2. Rabbi Jonathan Sacks
   "The Necessity of Asking Questions"
   Chabad.org
   The Chabad-Lubavitch Media Center
   https://www.Chabad.org/parshah/article_cdo/aid/3574984/Jewish/The-Necessity-of-Asking-Questions.htm
3. Genesis 26:7
4. Genesis 12:13 and 20:2
5. Genesis 18:12-15

6.   Genesis 27:18-19
7.   Genesis 27:6-17
8.   Genesis 27:1
9.   Genesis 35:28-29
10. In Genesis 27:46, Rebekah had indeed expressed self-preservation concerns in saying that she was "weary of [her] life" over the decisions of her son, Jacob— in addition to her previous concerns about Esau. She seemed to have a lack of confidence in the ability or willingness of either of her sons to care for her in her old age.
11. Genesis 27:6-17
12. Genesis 27:13
13. Genesis 27:27-29
14. Genesis 27:43-44
15. Genesis 28-31
16. Genesis 32:9
17. Genesis 32:24-30
18. Genesis 35:29
19. Genesis 27:1,19
20. Genesis 27:26-36
21. Genesis 4:4-8
22. Genesis 37:18-21
23. Genesis 37:31-34
24. Genesis 46:29

CHAPTER TWELVE
1.   Jared C. Pistoia, ND
     "Humor as a Coping Mechanism"
     PsychCentral – Updated June 28, 2022
     Healthline Media
     https://PsychCentral.com/lib/humor-as-weapon-shield-and-psychological-salve
2.   Genesis 13:5
3.   Taneasha White
     "Is It Possible to Repress Trauma?"
     PsychCentral – May 13, 2022
     Healthline Media
     https://PsychCentral.com/ptsd/repressed-trauma
4.   Genesis 19:2
5.   Genesis 19:4-5
6.   Genesis 19:6-7
7.   Genesis 19:8
8.   Tamar Kadari
     "Lot's Daughters: Midrash and Aggadah"
     The Shalvi/Hyman Encyclopedia of Jewish Women
     https://JWA.org/encyclopedia/article/lots-daughters-midrash-and-aggadah
9.   Genesis 19:32

10. Genesis 19:36
11. *"Fast Facts: Preventing Child Sexual Abuse"*
    Centers for Disease Control and Prevention (CDC) – Reviewed April 6, 2022
    U.S. Department of Health & Human Services (HHS)
    https://www.CDC.gov/violenceprevention/childsexualabuse/fastfact.html

CHAPTER THIRTEEN

1. Menachem Posner
   "Moses: The Biblical Prophet and Lawgiver Known as Moshe"
   Chabad.org
   The Chabad Lubavitch Media Center
   https://www.Chabad.org/library/article_cdo/aid/73398/Jewish/Moses.htm
2. Exodus 1:15-16
3. Exodus 1:17
4. Menachem Posner
   "Moses: The Biblical Prophet and Lawgiver Known as Moshe"
   Chabad.org
   The Chabad Lubavitch Media Center
   https://www.Chabad.org/library/article_cdo/aid/73398/Jewish/Moses.htm
5. Exodus 2:5-10
6. Numbers 27:1-4
7. Numbers 27:5-8
8. Exodus 15:20
9. Acts 7:22
10. Exodus 2:11
11. Exodus 2:11-12
12. Exodus 2:13-14
13. Exodus 2:15
14. Exodus 2:15
15. The Pharaoh, Seti I, is said to have died c. 1279 B.C.E. He was succeeded by his son, Rameses II. As Seti's son, Rameses would be a brother of Bithiah, Moses' adoptive Egyptian mother.
    Encyclopedia Britannica
    https://www.Britannica.com/biography/Seti-I
16. Exodus 3:2
17. Exodus 3:3
18. Exodus 4:10
19. Exodus 4:21
20. Scripture tells us that Moses actually expressed this fear to God in his first conversation with him. Exodus 3:11-14.
21. Exodus 4:10-16
22. Exodus 5:1-13
23. Exodus 5:19-21
24. Exodus 5:22-23
25. Exodus 6:1
26. Exodus 4:24

Notes
Pages 121 through 131

27. Exodus 4:24-26
28. Numbers 12:1-2
29. Numbers 12:2
30. Exodus 2:4
31. Deuteronomy 34:4
32. Numbers 12:3

CHAPTER FOURTEEN

1. Chana Weisberg
   "Nitzevet, Mother of David: The Bold Voice of Silence"
   The Jewish Woman
   https://www.Chabad.org/theJewishWoman/article_cdo/aid/280331/
   Jewish/Nitzevet-Mother-of-David.htm
2. Ibid.
3. 1 Samuel 16:17-18
4. Psalm 27:10
5. Psalm 68:5
6. 1 Samuel 17
7. 1 Samuel 17:17
8. 1 Samuel 17:18
9. 1 Samuel 17:8
10. 1 Samuel 17:32-37
11. 1 Samuel 17:22
12. 1 Samuel 17:42-44
13. 1 Samuel 16:11
14. 1 Samuel 17:40,49-50
15. 1 Samuel 17:38-42
16. 1 Samuel 17:39
17. 1 Samuel 17:49
18. 1 Samuel 17:49
19. 1 Samuel 17:49
20. 1 Samuel 17:51
21. The psalms attributed to David are: 3-9, 11-41, 51-65, 68-70, 86, 101, 103, 108-110, 122, 124, 131, 133, 138-145.
22. *"The Four Noble Truths"*
   BBC – Updated November 17, 2009
   https://www.BBC.co.uk/religion/religions/buddhism/beliefs/
   fournobletruths_1.shtml
23. Ibid.

CHAPTER FIFTEEN

1. Jesus read from Isaiah 61:1-2
2. *"The Incarnation"*
   The Catholic Encyclopedia
   New Advent
   https://www.NewAdvent.org/cathen/07706b.htm

203

Notes

3.   Catechism of the Catholic Church, paragraphs 1854-1864
     http://www.SCBorromeo.org/ccc/p3s1c1a8.htm#1854

4.   Nathan H. Lents, Ph.D.
     "The Beauty of Human Imperfection"
     Psychology Today – November 12, 2018
     https://www.PsychologyToday.com/us/blog/beastly-behavior/201811/the-beauty-human-imperfection

5.   Despite the Roman Catholic dogma of the Perpetual Virginity of Mary—that Mary was ever-virgin, and that she had no other children other than Jesus— Scripture clearly states that Jesus had siblings. *Matthew 12:47; Matthew 13:55-56; Mark 3:31; Mark 6:3; Luke 8:19; Galatians 1:19.* Scripture does not say that Mary was ever virgin. Scripture says that Mary and Joseph did not have sexual intimacy until after Jesus was born. *Matthew 1:25.*

6.   Ibid.

7.   Catechism of the Catholic Church, paragraph 2484.
     http://www.scborromeo.org/ccc/para/2484.htm

8.   Ibid.

9.   D. Moody Smith
     "Judaism and the Gospel of John"
     Boston College
     https://www.BC.edu/content/dam/files/research_sites/cjl/sites/partners/cbaa_seminar/Smith.htm

10. John 1:19; 2:18; 3:25; 5:15,18; 6:41,52; 7:1,11,15,35; 8:22,52,57; 9:18,22; 10:24,31; 11:8,33,36,45,54-55; 12:9,11 13:33; 18:31,38; 19:7,12,31,38

11. To be fair, Jesus did seem to have great respect for women. And women were among his biggest supporters. *Luke 8:2-3.*

12. See note 3 from Chapter Eight.

13. See Chapter Three.

14. *"The Scribes"*
     Bible.org
     https://Bible.org/seriespage/7-scribes

15. Mahatma Gandhi
     "What Jesus Means to Me" – Chapter 2: The Sermon on The Mount
     Gandhi Sevagram Ashram
     https://www.GandhiAshramSevagram.org/what-jesus-means-to-me/sermon-on-the-mount.php

16. Scripture tells us in Luke 2:52 that Jesus grew wiser with age. This means that, like anyone else, he learned from his parents and others, he learned from his experiences, and he was wiser as an adult than he was as a child or an adolescent. Whatever else we may believe about the divinity of Christ, Jesus was one hundred percent human.

17. Ibid.

18. Mark 6:3

19. Scripture tells us in Matthew 1:18-19 that, upon hearing that Mary was pregnant, Joseph initially sought to part ways with her thinking that she had committed sexual sin. Joseph believed that Mary had committed the sin of

fornication until, according to Matthew 1:20, an angel told Joseph that Mary's child had been conceived by the Holy Spirit.

20. These rumors are, of course, speculation by the author and others. It is logical, though, to assume such rumors happened as it is unlikely that the belief in the virgin birth was known and accepted by the people of Nazareth back then, and word of an unmarried young woman getting pregnant would have been a source of scandal to them.

21. Scripture tells us in John 8:41 that, during the course of an argument or debate with Jesus, someone felt the need to point out to Jesus that they were not born illegitimately. This has been interpreted as an *ad hominem* attack against the questionable paternity of Jesus. Scripture also tells us in Mark 6:3 that Jesus was referred to as "the Son of Mary" by people in his hometown of Nazareth rather than the son of Joseph.

———

Bruce Chilton
"The Mamzer Jesus and His Birth"
The Bible and Interpretation | The University of Arizona – October 2005
https://bibleinterp.Arizona.edu/articles/2005/10/chi298001

22. John 8:2-11
23. Deuteronomy 23:23-24
24. Luke 2:49,52
25. Luke 2:41-52
26. Luke 2:46
27. Luke 2:49
28. The Bible is silent as to whatever became of Joseph. All that is clear from Scripture is that Joseph seems to be out of the picture by the time Jesus was crucified. Many Christians have long speculated that Joseph must have passed away at some point between the time Jesus was twelve years old (see Luke 2:41-42), and the time of the Crucifixion. This statement is in accord with that speculation.

———

"Joseph (father of Jesus)"
New World Encyclopedia
https://www.NewWorldEncyclopedia.org/entry/Joseph_(father_of_Jesus)

29. Scripture tells us in Luke 1:36, 63 that Elizabeth, the mother of John the Baptist, was a relative of Mary, probably a cousin. Luke 3:1-3 tells us that John was called by God and was widely known.
30. Matthew 14:3-4; Mark 6:17-18
31. John 1:27
32. Mark 1:9
33. Matthew 14:10
34. Matthew 5:48
35. Luke 4:3-4
36. Luke 4:5-8
37. Scripture tells us in Hebrews 4:15 that, while Jesus never sinned, he was "in all points tempted like as we are."

Notes

38. Scripture never tells us that Jesus questioned why God allowed him to be tempted by the devil in the desert. However, this statement reflects the author's speculation that, perhaps, Jesus may have inwardly and silently questioned God's will occasionally before he vocally questioned God's will while on the Cross. Matthew 27:46; Mark 15:34.

39. Luke 22:42

40. Jesus was as capable of feeling anxiety as anyone else. Scripture tells us in Luke 22:44 that, while he prayed in the Garden of Gethsemane, he was in "agony" and was so filled with stress and anxiety that "his sweat became like drops of blood falling on the ground."

41. This statement reflects the author's speculation that, perhaps, Jesus may have inwardly and silently questioned God's will occasionally before he vocally questioned God's will while on the Cross. Matthew 27:46; Mark 15:34

42. Matthew 26:36-46; Mark 14:32-42; Luke 22:39-46.

43. Luke 22:44

44. Luke 22:43-44

45. According to Scripture, in Matthew 27:46 and Mark 15:34, Jesus did in fact feel forsaken, i.e., abandoned, by God.

46. John 19:30

47. According to Scripture, in Matthew 27:46 and Mark 15:34, Jesus did in fact feel forsaken, i.e., abandoned, by God.

48. Matthew 27:29

49. According to Scripture, in Matthew 27:46 and Mark 15:34, Jesus did in fact feel forsaken, i.e., abandoned, by God.

50. During his days on this earth, Jesus was not omniscient. In light of Luke 2:52, which tells us that Jesus grew wiser with age, it is not improper to suggest that Jesus developed deeper understandings about life as the result of his experiences.

51. Luke 23:35

52. Luke 23:34

53. Luke 23:34

54. John 1:29

55. John 19:28

56. Throughout Scripture, whenever Jesus addresses or refers to God as "Father," he uses the Aramaic word *abba*, which is an intimate term such as a child would use to address his or her Daddy. It is this intimate trusting term that Jesus did not use while addressing God in his final words on the Cross, according to Matthew and Mark.

Chris Sustar
"Abba, Father"
Evangel Magazine
Church of God Publications – October 4, 2017
https://www.EvangelMagazine.com/2017/10/abba-father/

57. Matthew 27:46

58. "St. Joan of Arc"

Notes
Pages 152 through 165

New Advent
Catholic Encyclopedia
https://www.NewAdvent.org/cathen/08409c.htm

59. Matthew 5:22,28,32,34,39,44; 11:24; 12:6,36; 17:12; 26:29; Mark 9:13; Luke 6:27; 10:12.

60. This new covenant was predicted—and quoted here in the New Testament without attribution—by the prophet Jeremiah. *Jeremiah 31:31-34.*

61. These commandments did not originate with Jesus. He drew from Deuteronomy 6:5 and Leviticus 19:18 to form what he considered to be the kernel of the law of God.

62. Sharon Martin, LCSW
    "What Is Self-Love and Why Is It So Important?"
    Psych Central – May 31, 2019
    Healthline Media
    https://PsychCentral.com/blog/imperfect/2019/05/what-is-self-love-and-why-is-it-so-important

63. *"A List of the 613 Mitzvot (Commandments)"*
    Judaism 101
    Tracey R. Rich
    https://www.JewFAQ.org/613_commandments

64. The sayings of Jesus in chapters 8, 10, 14, and 15 of the Gospel of John "sound" like they are post-resurrectional. It is possible that someone felt that the Risen Jesus spoke these words to them, and then they inserted them into the Gospel as if spoken by the historical Jesus. This is beyond the scope of this book. The reader is invited to look into this further for themselves.

65. Genesis 7:17-21

66. Exodus 12:29-30

67. Lisa Webber
    "25 Bible Passages About Plagues and Pestilence"
    The Christian Broadcasting Network
    https://www1.CBN.com/bible-passages-about-plagues-and-pestilence/spiritual-life

68. See note 3 from Chapter Eight

69. Genesis 19:24-24

70. Joshua 11:18-23

71. *"Act of God"*
    Law Insider Dictionary
    https://www.LawInsider.com/dictionary/act-of-god

72. Ibid.

73. Deshlee Ford
    "Reparenting Your Inner Child: Ways to Encourage Therapeutic Dialogue"
    Step Up For Mental Health – July 16, 2021
    https://www.StepUpForMentalHealth.org/reparenting-your-inner-child/

74. Ibid.

75. Sharon Martin, LCSW
    "Learn to Reparent Yourself"

Notes
Pages 165 through 188

Psych Central – November 22, 2019
Healthline Media
https://PsychCentral.com/blog/imperfect/2019/11/learn-to-reparent-yourself

76. Deshlee Ford
"Reparenting Your Inner Child: Ways to Encourage Therapeutic Dialogue"
Step Up For Mental Health – July 16, 2021
https://www.StepUpForMentalHealth.org/reparenting-your-inner-child/

CHAPTER SIXTEEN
1. Romans, 1 Corinthians, 2 Corinthians, Galatians, Ephesians, Philippians, Colossians, 1 Thessalonians, 2 Thessalonians, 1 Timothy, 2 Timothy, Titus, Philemon
2. The Bible tells a story about how God teaches Peter that Gentile Christians should not be required to keep all of the provisions of the Mosaic law. *Acts 10:9-11:18.*
3. *"New Testament Word No. 4567"*
Strong's Biblical Concordance
https://BibleHub.com/greek/4657.htm

AFTERWORD
1. Anthony Orlando
"The 10 Most Popular Movies of All Time, Ranked by Box Office Gross"
Digital Trends Media Group
https://www.DigitalTrends.com/movies/the-10-most-popular-movies-of-all-time-ranked-by-adjusted-worldwide-box-office-gross/
2. Benedict Carey
"Who's Minding the Mind?"
The New York Times – July 31, 2007
https://www.NYTimes.com/2007/07/31/health/psychology/31subl.html
3. Hilary I. Lebow
"Self-Sabotage: Why You Hold Yourself Back"
PsychCentral – Updated November 5, 2021
Healthline Media
https://PsychCentral.com/blog/overcome-self-sabotage
4. Taneasha White
"Is It Possible to Repress Trauma?"
Psych Central – May 13, 2022
Healthline Media
https://PsychCentral.com/ptsd/repressed-trauma
5. Christopher Bergland
"Unconscious Memories Hide in the Brain but Can Be Retrieved"
Psychology Today – August 17, 2015
https://www.PsychologyToday.com/us/blog/the-athletes-way/201508/unconscious-memories-hide-in-the-brain-can-be-retrieved
6. *"We Have Met the Enemy and He Is Us"*

Notes
Page 188

Billy Ireland Cartoon Library & Museum
University Libraries
The Ohio State University
https://library.OSU.edu/site/40stories/2020/01/05/we-have-met-the-enemy/

www.ingramcontent.com/pod-product-compliance
Lightning Source LLC
Chambersburg PA
CBHW060845280326
41934CB00007B/920